BUTTA
The First 15 Years

Joey "Butta" Mazza

Fulton Books
Meadville, PA

Published by Fulton Books 2023

What you are about to read is all true,
except for the parts that aren't.

ISBN 979-8-88731-050-3 (paperback)
ISBN 979-8-88731-051-0 (digital)

Printed in the United States of America

Dedicated to all the Wingmen who came before me and to all the Wingmen to follow. It is every Wingmen's duty and honor to reach the Wall.

WFFW RFFDD

FOREWORD

This is the story of how I became a Wingmen and the tales of my most memorable trips both good and bad times to date in the Wingmen Motorcycle Club.

If you bought this book expecting to hear about crazy club on club shoot-outs, rape, drug deals, or pimping ole ladies, sorry, you bought the wrong book. Now let me make a few things perfectly clear: we are not a 1 percent club, but we aren't your local HOG chapter or weekend-riding club either. Yes, this club started out as a "military" club, with its roots going back to the midseventies in Italy and finally becoming the Wingmen Motorcycle Club July 4, 1979, in Fayetteville, North Carolina. But back then the brothers that started or were there at the beginning when the club started to grow, Patrick Murphy, Mike Roy, Bill Beard, John Humphreys, Lee Carrillo, Scar, and Joe "JD" Dwyer, to name the core, fought their asses off to get the respect and were able to hold that respect to be able to survive and thrive into the nation we have become today.

They did things according to tradition. There were no "patching over" or purchasing colors for a couple hundred bucks through an e-mail. They didn't wear original eight patches. None of them claimed to be our "owner" or grand puba.

They followed motorcycle club protocol that was established before them. No one got a free ride; you had to earn it through prospecting no matter who you were or who you knew. The club was tested early on in Columbus, Georgia, and a prominent 1 percent club found out real fast the Wingmen will not be told what to do where to do it or to support any other club. They also found out the

Wingmen bite back just as hard, if not harder. Those brothers earned respect putting in work and spilling sweat and blood.

Their message was simple: Don't fuck with us, and we won't fuck with you. Leave us alone, and we leave you alone. We have always and will always be independent. We are men and will be treated as such. We will treat others like men in return if there is a mutual respect. We consider ourselves at eye level unless you force us to look down on you.

Most of our members fought for your American rights. One of them is to act like an asshole, just don't do it around us or toward us.

You don't see too much of that anymore. The loyalty for one's club has all but gone. You meet some patch holder from a club, and a few months later, he is wearing a different patch, and so on. A lot of the bigger 1 percent clubs are now selling out for membership, watering down requirements, taking others' quitters and/or out bad and/or just outright selling their patches to whomever wants to wear them. These tactics were introduced in 2004 by a club that flashed onto the scene in middle America and grew to, like, a hundred chapters within a few years. They have since split into about four other clubs and have been the center of many protocol arguments, almost all their "original eight" members claiming ownership of their newest Ponzi scheme club.

Don't get me wrong, we have had our share of quitters and guys that got expelled as well. No organization is ever going to have 100 percent happy or great members. But to get the opportunity to be one of us and then get the chance to be expelled or quit, you had to earn your patch first.

It is sad to see our lifestyle slowing eating itself. Anyway, I just wanted to make it perfectly clear how this club earned it and how we still hold true to that process decades later.

INTRODUCTION

My name is Joey Mazza. My friends and brothers know me as "Butta." This is the story of how and why I became a Wingmen. It also tells the tales of my most memorable road trips that I have logged while riding close to three hundred thousand miles with my patch on my back in the fifteen years of me being a Wingmen thus far. Back when I was a new patch holder in early 2007, I met our founding father, Patrick Murphy. He gave me great advice on how to be a Wingmen for the rest of my life. He also told me to keep a log of every trip I take. He said, "Later on in life, if you ever wanted to write a book, it makes life a hell of a lot easier." He then told me he was writing a book at the time and didn't keep a log, and it was a nightmare trying to recount all his travels and good times with the club. Well, Murph finished his book, and it was awesome, and it was an inspiration for me years later to write this. I hope you enjoy it as much as I did his. Murph's book is called *Good Bikes, Good Friends, Good Times and Baaaddddd Women!*

Another brother by the name of John Humphreys wrote a book called *On Eagles Wings*. If you haven't read them, you need to. These books let you know how the club started in Verona, Italy, in the 1970s and how that led to the expansion into the United States beginning in Fayetteville July 4, 1979. Two great reads from two great Wingmen and brothers.

Some things to note, it is a kutte, not cut. The word originated decades ago in our Biker Culture. A kutte is a battle jacket. It was born from combat. It was adopted in the biker culture because it is usually adorned with club paraphernalia and has given its wearer the sense of protection. That is the story I got many, many years ago through the old bikers that were in my life, so that is the way I will spell it in this book.

Also, I don't use P. The word is fucking president. So it will be spelled out. To me, being called a P is insulting and disrespectful. I loved the show *Sons of Anarchy* (yes, I did, it was very entertaining), but that show is the reason everyone all of a sudden uses P.

WFFW 9339 RFFDD

CHAPTER 1

I was born October 29, 1964. I grew up in a city by the name of Garfield in northeastern New Jersey. Garfield was split down the railroad tracks. The north side was all Italian, and the south was all Polish. Till I was seven, I had no "man of the house" in my home. My mother raised my older sister, Vicki, and myself. My dad split when I was like one. My father's family surrounded our house, and I still saw my grandmother and grandfather who lived right around the block. My grandfather's brother, my uncle Dominic, was right next to them. His brother, my uncle Leo, was only a few blocks away, and my grandmother's three brothers were all just as close. Back then, family didn't move far apart from each other.

When I was seven, my mom started dating a man named Jack. He had five kids from a previous marriage who would become my stepsisters and brothers. I also had a half sister and brother from my biological father's second marriage (though I really never saw them unless they were visiting our grandmother).

Anyway, I won't bore you with my upbringing. The only story I want to tell here is about my tenth birthday. My stepfather, Jack, was into horses, and for my tenth birthday, he bought me a horse. A beautiful Appaloosa named Fox. Well, my biological father was dating some young Playboy bunny from the Playboy club in Vernon, New Jersey (true story). She was young, hot, and dreamed of a family and kids. So my biological decides he will use my sisters, my brother, and I as props that year to reel her in. That year was the most I'd ever spent with him when I was a child.

When he caught wind of my gift from Jack, he had to one-up my stepfather. So he bought me a brand-new 1974 Harley-Davidson Z90. I know what you're all thinking: *Best birthday ever!* It was. What my biological didn't know was, Jack was into bikes as well and had a 1971 Harley-Davidson FLH in my garage. So with the Z90 and Jack's guidance, along with a lot of road rash, broken bones, and stitches, I learned to ride. The hook was set.

CHAPTER 2

Fierce Allegiance and the Northern Alliance

Before becoming a Wingmen, I was in another motorcycle club. Their name was Fierce Allegiance. We were also out of Bergen County, New Jersey. Bergen County is a large county. We were based out of Oakland, which is northwest of my home. We were a one-chapter club, a bunch of guys that were pretty tight. Our MO was to basically go to bars frequented by illegal immigrants, instigate a fight, and beat up on them.

Now, I'm not saying it was a good thing to do or the right thing to do—definitely not the politically correct thing to do—but it humored us, and it gave us something to do. Besides, most of them (the immigrants) welcomed the fight.

We were a part of approximately fifteen or so other clubs that called ourselves the Northern Alliance. We kind of acted like a nation in the MC world. If you fought one patch in the Northern Alliance, you fought all the patches in the Northern Alliance. The Northern Alliance was put together basically to keep the clubs involved out of 1 percent politics. New Jersey is a highly active MC state. Most MCs were "supporting" one of the two dominant 1 percent clubs in the state, whether they wanted to or not. So we as members of the Northern Alliance would meet once a month with all MC presidents and any members who wanted to attend. The presidents would give an area report and schedule parties and events and so forth. The Northern Alliance representative would then meet with both 1 percent clubs and keep them up to speed with what we were doing and where. We didn't invite them to our stuff, and we did not want to attend theirs.

The man that represented the Northern Alliance in public and who presided over our meetings was a president of a one-chapter club in northwestern New Jersey. I'll call him Jim. I won't use real names as to protect the innocent and all. Jim was a very small older guy, but a lot of the Northern Alliance members looked up to him because he looked and lived the part of a "real biker." He was complete with old faded tattoos, ponytail, and weathered leather skin from decades of riding. He was a soft-spoken guy; very rarely did he raise his voice or leave even keel. I'll give credit where it is due and say he was a biker through and through. He also was a guy who commanded respect and definitely got it from most. His club followed suit and were the grungiest of the Northern Alliance. They were the biggest, and though never really tested, I'd be pressed to say they were probably, as a whole, the toughest.

All was great in the Northern Alliance world for a while. We all got along. We all supported each other's parties and runs. There wasn't any in fighting except for the usual drunken biker beer and testosterone-fueled melee. Then a large number of one of the dominant 1 percent club's members all got out of jail at the same time (most of them went away at the same time for the same incident). That's when Jim started acting more and more like he picked a side.

The two 1 percent clubs started clashing, and they both started pressing clubs from the Northern Alliance to join their "coalitions." Some of the clubs caved out of fear or just had the 1 percent envy, as I like to call it.

Let me get something straight, I have nothing against 1 percent clubs. I respect their commitment to their way of life no matter the consequences. They paved the way for the biker society as we know it today. They stood up to every obstacle thrown at them and came out bigger and stronger just about every time.

What I do have a problem with is someone wanting to have the clout of the 1 percenter via coattails. In my encounters over the decades that I have been involved with in the MC society, that is *my opinion* from experience. If you want to be a 1 percenter, more power to you. If you want to support a 1 percent club, more power to you. However, if you want to act like one and command the respect of one by thinking being a "supporter" is your avenue to do so, well, that isn't going to fly with me. Never did, never will.

Back to Jim. At around the same time, Jim started acting like he didn't have the Northern Alliance's best interests in mind with some of his decisions. His plans for the future of the Northern Alliance were questionable at the least. I voiced my opinion to my president, and it was clear he wasn't going to ask any questions and just fall in line and follow. That left a bad taste in my mouth.

I then went to a couple brothers with whom I was closest with and voiced my concerns to them. Some saw what I did. Some saw it as our president's way of saying, let's keep out of their business.

It was the spring of 2005 when it was becoming clearer what Jim's intentions were. He was all but outright politicking for one side in the battle for New Jersey. The Northern Alliance started breaking down. One by one clubs fell to the pressure of support. Fierce Allegiance held fast and would not fall to the pressure. We had a few scuffles here and there with the new "coalition" clubs from both sides. We lost some of what we had thought were friendships along the way. But all in all, I was very proud to be a part of a club that refused to support out of fear.

Tensions between myself and our president were mounting. Myself and some brothers talked about breaking off and starting another chapter. It made sense and would've been a good move. We had the bodies to do so, and it would've given us the separation some of us needed and would've expanded our recruiting area.

It was talked about in just about every church, and arguments would end up shutting down the discussion. It was very clear our president wasn't sharing his power with anyone or was willing to change with the times for the club's future.

The following Northern Alliance meeting the Wingmen MC was brought up in discussion. It was believed at the time that they were a support club for the 1 percent club that presided in northeastern New Jersey. No one really had any intel on them, so we couldn't make an educated guess on the speculation. We all heard of them in Rockland, New York, but weren't sure if this was the same club and branched out into New Jersey. Jim then asked if anyone wanted to attend a party the Wingmen had been advertising the following weekend. He wanted a few members from a few different Northern Alliance clubs to attend and gather intel. My hand went up immediately. I was eager to find out who these Wingmen were, especially since they were right in my backyard.

My president as usual wasn't too happy with me volunteering and voiced his opinion to me. My "half" of the club really wasn't paying too much mind to him at this point, and it showed. He was pissed 'cause now he had to go too. He wasn't going to let me go it alone.

CHAPTER 3

Finally Meet the New Jersey Wingmen

Myself, president, two other patch holders, along with a prospect were going. The following Saturday night, we rolled into the Elks Lodge in Hasbrouck Heights. The place was packed, and the first thing I noticed was a ton of out-of-state plates on most of the bikes there. Also noticed there were none of the 1 percent club members there that they supposedly supported.

We paid our $20 at the door (Kenny still only $20 after all these years! We need to increase that!) and did our usual scan the room look for exits, cameras, etc. We met up with a few other Northern Alliance members that volunteered to go, and it was confirmed there were no members of alleged 1 percent club there. But maybe they were to show up later; sometimes they like making grand entrances.

I started making mental notes of all the bottom rockers this club, the Wingmen, were sporting, and it came to me very early: this was no support club. Fayetteville; Savannah, Georgia; Orange County, New York; Rockland County, New York; Phenix City, Alabama; Opelika, Alabama; Devil's Elbow, Missouri; Oak Grove, Kentucky; Effingham County, Georgia; Moore County, North Carolina; North Georgia; Long County, Georgia; and Northeast Georgia. To go along with the Bergen County, New Jersey, rocker.

Now, this is where I met a man who would become one of my best friends and whom I consider my family. I can honestly say, if not for him, I doubt I would be a Wingmen.

The Wingmen rockers aren't that easy to read with the wedding text and all. So a Wingmen with what turned out to be a Georgia bottom rocker walked by. At the time, I honestly couldn't tell if the GA after the Long County was for Georgia or California. I stopped him and introduced myself. We shook hands. His name was CC. He was a stocky guy with reddish-blond crew cut. He was heavily inked and was visibly halfway to meeting his goal of being drunk. Those who know brother CC well know the next part as no surprise. When my prospect who was at my side introduced himself and extended his hand, he was met with a "yeah" and a half-hearted handshake.

I said, "I have to ask you a question, and don't take it as disrespect, but is that GA for Georgia, or is it CA for California?" (We didn't wear chapter bars back then.)

CC looked me dead in the eyes all serious and said, "Now, if I were from California, I'd be gay and walk and talk funny."

I thought to myself, *Here we go, Butta. Now you're going to have to fight this dude*, thinking he took offense to my question.

Then he busted out laughing and looked at me and said, "Don't even say I walk funny!"

We laughed, and I sent the prospect to get us some drinks and then dismissed him to find our president and cover him.

CC introduced me to a brother of his, Country, also from Long County. Then to a brother named PD from Long County as well. They (Country and PD) also happened to be blood brothers as well as club brothers.

I couldn't make out a word PD was trying to say all night. I was not fluent in nighttime PD as of yet. Country, CC, and myself talked for a few hours, and that impressed me. Gotta figure, with them being around nine hundred miles south of here, they probably don't get to see most of their brothers often; and yet they took the time to talk to another patch and make him feel at home.

CC and I exchanged numbers and said our goodbyes. I found my president at the bar with my other brothers and a few patches from the Northern Alliance.

I ordered a last beer and looked at my president and said, "Well, I think it's safe to say they aren't a support club, and I had a great fucking time. They are squared away and have some pretty cool members."

My president looked at me and said, "Yeah, just don't go changing back patches on me."

I paid the comment no mind at the time. Coming from him, I didn't take offense to it 'cause his opinion meant nothing to me. From another member and we probably would've been rolling on the floor. Little did I know that he took more from my experience there than I did.

A funny sidenote: Bergen gave away a ticket for door prizes with your entry fee. I won a $100 gift certificate to a local tattoo shop. That is, to date, the only thing I have ever won at a Wingmen event! So stop trying to sell me raffle tickets. *I don't win!*

CHAPTER 4

Standing Down

CC and I talked all the time on the phone. To the point where I trusted him enough to talk to him about my dilemma with my club. On one side, there was me and half the club looking at me for guidance, and on the other was our president who wouldn't budge on any of the change we brought to the table.

It was his club, and he was not going to move an inch. Mostly on spite, I think, because the requests for change were all good requests. We didn't have a clubhouse. We had a local bar that we basically did anything we wanted to with it. Having a party, we would close it down to anyone not invited or willing to pay to enter that night. We held our meetings in a back room, and it was off-limits to anyone who wasn't a patch holder. One of the requests was to get an actual clubhouse. Another was to expand our area of operation and to break off to a Passaic County chapter. That would've put us right over the river from Bergen County's southwest side. All fell on deaf ears, and all were the right moves to make for the club at that critical time.

I confided in CC. I have to say, I was surprised he never once said, "Fuck that guy. Why don't you become a Wingmen?" And to be honest, that wasn't my thoughts or intentions at the time. CC gave me solid advice on how he would handle the situation, and I tried a lot of what he said. To no avail, President and his side wouldn't budge. This went on for around eight months. President and I went back and forth, back and forth. This went on to the point, the two halves of the club were about to have it out in a parking lot, winner take all.

I truly in my heart didn't want that to happen. After a lot of soul-searching and talking with my brothers who believed in me, myself and a few others decided it would be best for us to step down and walk away. We knew President was never going to change or give up his stranglehold. He had us in numbers by a few and would win anything brought put to a vote. His side would never let our side patch someone in that would vote our way. So it was a no-win situation.

It's funny 'cause, in trying times, you find out who your true brothers are. There were seven of us and a prospect who were fighting President and nine others. Only two of us with the prospect ended up walking away. Their reasons varied, but I know they all wanted to keep a patch on their backs and didn't want to start over and have to prospect with another club.

CHAPTER 5

Hanging Around

I was immediately courted by a host of other clubs both in the Northern Alliance and outside of it. Some went as far as to offer me a patch on the spot. They lost what respect I may have had for them by offering that to me.

Becoming part of a club is a rite of passage. Over the years, you always see the same shit. Four to ten guys just binge-watched *Sons of Anarchy* or *Gangland* and get the bright idea to start a club. Complete with "original eight" or "first six" patches. Always makes me laugh.

If you are looking to be a patch holder in a club, you should find the right club for you and help strengthen it. One that has the same values and beliefs as you. Then you hang around them to be sure you are right for them and they are right for you. Then you ask to prospect, and hopefully, you patch out. It's best to find the right club and strengthen their numbers than to start a silly club with you and your lazy, scared-to-prospect "brothers" that won't be around for more than three years. Just my opinion.

I did check out some of the local clubs that I knew to be pretty strong and on the right path. But none of them could offer me what the Wingmen offered me. Thousands of miles between clubhouses, and from what I had seen in CC, PD, and Country so far, real brotherhood. They were a nation spread out up and down the East Coast and Middle America.

They at the time had fourteen chapters and one probate chapter (Calhoun County, Alabama). From New York to Georgia to Missouri. That is what I needed, and that is what I wanted. I called CC and asked him to get me in contact with the Bergen County chapter. He asked me if I was sure this was what I wanted. He stressed to me the level of commitment the Wingmen nation demanded from their patch holders. He also reminded me that he was vouching for me, and I better not make a fool of him for his decision. I told him, "That's what I'm looking to find out. If I did this, I wouldn't let him down. But I won't know if I don't meet them and hang out with them."

CC contacted Bermuda Mike. He was Bergen's president at the time. Mike had CC give me his contact information. Myself and my prospect from Fierce Allegiance, "Styx," made plans to go meet them at their clubhouse before their church that Friday night.

That Friday Styx and I rolled up to the Wingmen clubhouse off green street in South Hackensack around 1800 hours. Everyone was outside, and handshakes and introductions were going around. Mike was a small guy, medium build, real clean-cut. I would've taken him for a lawyer or business guy if he were dressed differently. Mike asked me about my time with Fierce Allegiance, and I told him what I deemed necessary. I didn't shit on them at all. I still had respect and love for a lot of them. Basically, just told him we had our differences and decided it was best if Styx and I parted ways. We were both out "good." Meaning we didn't owe money, we didn't lie, steal, or disrespect the club.

Mike, Styx, and I sat down inside the clubhouse and shot the shit. Mike had told me CC spoke highly of me and now that we know where they are to come around if we wanted, never bringing up prospecting or anything about the club. Just said we were to come around if we wanted to and to get to know the members.

Mike had an amazing confidence about him. For a guy who is probably five foot seven first thing in the morning and maybe a buck sixty, he carried himself like he was ten feet tall with a battle-ax in both hands. That day I met Little Kenny, Igor, Darren, Ronnie, Phil, Frankie the Elbow, Old-man Rick, Barry, LaRock, and Charlie

Balls. Everyone was pretty receptive. We bullshitted and had a few beers, then they resided inside for church. Afterward we all rode to a bar, Angie B'z, in Elmwood Park. Styx and I stayed for a while then headed out. Before leaving, I exchanged numbers with a few of the guys.

This went on for a few weeks, and the chapter was having their spring breakout run. They get together with the Rockland and Orange County chapters, go for a ride, and make sure everyone's bikes are up to par and all proper paperwork is in order for the year.

I immediately grabbed the spatula from Phil and manned the grill. I helped as much as I could and also stayed back from the ride to get the food all ready for their return. Styx, on the other hand, started drinking and went on the run.

I met most of the Rockland and Orange brothers that day: Rockland prospect, Johnny Crash, and Orange County's prospect Chaz; Randy, Chachie, Tommy Turmoil, Little Jimmy, Odd Todd, Little Brian, Brain, JD, Johnny Love, Nole, Fireman John, Talking John, Dozer, No-Hurry Murry, Karate Joe, Eric Taddio, Belaby, Big Willie, Matsuyi, McGuiness, Billy Man; Orange County prospects ED and Tommy Pipe; and one of the greatest Wingmen ever, Curtis.

Now a lot of those names from Bergen, Rockland, and Orange counties a lot of you brothers won't recognize. Most of them aren't Wingmen anymore. Some are dead and on the GBNF wall. Some are just dead. I choose to mention any and all that were Wingmen 'cause they all were once one of us, and it is a good reminder that if you fuck up, you may end up like one of them. Not all fucked up. Some woke up one day and decided this isn't what they wanted anymore. Most of them were usually subpar Wingmen to begin with. It amazes me sometimes the guys that fake it long enough to get patched then become a drunken piece of shit. Others leave under pressure, usually an ole lady ultimatum. Either way, they left. Some have made me happy they are no longer with us; others have broken my heart. However, they are all part of our club's past, whether we like it or not.

I want to talk a little about brother Curtis from Rockland County. Curtis was young, early twenties, when he prospected. The story goes, at first, no one really took Curtis seriously. He was about five foot ten inches and somewhere in the buck fifty-to-sixty range. He looked like he was twelve years old.

Curtis suffered from cystic fibrosis. His physical abilities were very limited, but his heart and love for this club and his brothers was insurmountable. The older Rockland guys can give you some great tales of Curtis. I have one myself. I was blessed with taking a road trip with Curtis to Alabama. It turned out to be his last. I will tell that tale a little later in the book. I suggest you get with some of the Rockland and Bergen brothers some time and listen and learn what a great Wingmen and brother Curtis was. He was a great brother and is sorely missed. More about Curtis later.

That day went well for me. I seemed to be accepted by everyone and started to forge some good relationships that day. At the end of the night, Mike asked me if I liked what I saw. I did. Everyone was genuinely receptive, and they all seemed to get along well. He told me they would be going to Rockland next Friday night for a special Wingmen-invite-only event and asked if I wanted to come.

"Sure," I said. "What time is kickstands up?"

"1800 hours" was his reply.

Styx wasn't invited.

The following Friday, I rolled up to the clubhouse, and most of the guys were there already. We had a few beers then hit the road to Rockland. One thing us northern brothers can always boast about is our riding skills in a pack. Most chapters are in the sticks and or in way smaller "cities" than ours. We ride tight, hard, and fast. We have to. You give any of the idiots up here more the three feet and they will nose their piece-of-shit uninsured car in the pack to try and save themselves ten seconds of travel time. So we hammered up to Rockland. The old firehouse clubhouse. I miss that house—too many memories to ever forget that place.

Around 2000 hours, Mike told me they were all going up stairs for church. I was left at the bar with Prospect Ed and Tommy Pipe, both from Orange County. We hung out and shot the shit, and they enjoyed the downtime of not having to tend to brothers. About for-ty-five minutes later, they all came filing back downstairs, only now

Johnny Crash and Chaz were full patch holders. They had earned their eagles that night.

That night I spent a lot of time talking with Tommy Turmoil. Tommy is one of the largest humans I've met to date face-to-face. My neck was killing me looking up at him for so long. But he gave me great insight on what I was getting myself into if I chose this path. I remember talking a lot with Odd Todd and Dozer as well. Todd is one of the most loyal brothers I have met over the years. We had a few "spats" over the years. But to this day, I have always defended Todd with saying, "If I called Todd at 0230 and told him I was in a bar and five bad guys just walked in, he would run in three minutes later in his tighty-whities and half a hard-on, ready to fight." Todd, I love you, brother, even when you thought I didn't.

At the end of the night, I approached Mike and asked him what I need to do to stand up. He told me get a vest and come to the clubhouse that next Friday night. I knew I would be standing up well before I asked and had a custom leather vest made at Passaic Leather weeks before. It is still in service to this day.

CHAPTER 6

Standing Up and Prospecting

The following Friday, I arrived at the clubhouse and went through the process of standing up. It was a proud moment because I knew this was the beginning of something way bigger than anything I have been a part of before. Like most of us, I was looking for something, wanting and needing to be a part of something I could be myself in and not be judged. I had a really fucked-up childhood and had major trust issues. I wanted to surround myself with a family who thought as I did and who saw the world as I did. I served in the Marine Corps Reserves and the National Guard. The Wingmen Motorcycle Club is predominantly a military club. At the time, we were probably 90 percent active or former military. Though the Bergen and New York chapters were more civilian, being Wingmen gave them a sense of military mindset and pride. I knew if I made it, I would have the whole Wingmen nation to envelope myself in not just the Bergen and New York chapters.

I was looking forward to the challenge and wanted deep within myself to be a part of it. Bergen was a probate chapter when it started. It was started with patch holders Darren, Ronnie, Frankie the Elbow, and Little Joe from Rockland. They started with thirteen probates. On June 2, 2006, the chapter voted me to be their first ever prospect.

I had prospected before and knew pretty much what to expect and how to handle myself. Later that night, we went to the Satans Soldiers New Jersey chapter's clubhouse. It felt good to introduce myself as "Butta, prospect, Wingmen Nation, New Jersey." Though most of the introductions weren't needed since I knew most of them already. I did it to make sure everyone knew the path I chose.

My prospecting time was a little mundane in the sense I was well schooled in the MC world and was well known and respected in the MC world that was our AO. But I was at the immediate beck and call of three chapters and had to learn the Wingmen way and the way the chapter and nation ran. I was in constant contact with CC, Country, PD, Ligget, and Doc Kipp. Doc was a brother out of our Savannah chapter, who was overseas in Iraq, contracting. We would e-mail back and forth. Ligget was out of Fayetteville, and he was deployed in Germany. I had made initial contact with them both through CC via phone calls when they were home on leave. We exchanged contact info, and we have been close brothers since. They helped me a lot with learning the Wingmen way.

Being close with CC was a good thing to have in my corner. He was the president of our Long County chapter, Georgia, and a highly respected brother throughout the nation. So when he would tell brothers, "This guy Butta prospecting for Bergen is a good dude," it had weight to it. If anything, it let patch holders know out of the gate I was squared away, "so don't be an ass to him."

Now, we don't shit on prospects as a club. I personally never understood some club's mentality with that. They are your "prospective" brother. Why would you want to humiliate them or embarrass them in front of others? Now, that doesn't mean we aren't hard on prospects; just saying we won't make you do something we (patch holders) wouldn't be doing right next to you or with you. I once was at another club's party in West Virginia, and they had a fucking cowbell on their prospect, and when he wasn't running errands, he had to hide out of sight! What the fuck?

I spent a lot of time at the Rockland and Orange clubhouses as well. When you prospect, you prospect for the nation, not just the chapter. For those that want to bitch and moan about your Wingmen-prospecting time, fuck you. I prospected when Rockland had no prospects, Orange had two, and one wasn't worth a shit. Then throw in the fact that Darren was recently divorced and a whole other Darren than you know now. Johnny Love was active. Chaz was just realizing he had an alter ego known as Nighttime Chaz. Johnny Crash never slept, ever. Randy had just discovered steroids. It was a five to six-day-a-week gig. Ed, prospect from Orange, and I were run ragged. Tommy was the piece of shit who was getting carried along. The two of us put in work a lot of work.

Rockland at that time had the absolute best killer parties hands down. They had been a chapter for eighteen years and had the area locked down with civilian support. Their first party I worked as a prospect late that June or early July. I smashed three broads, two upstairs in Johnny Love's room and one in the closet under the staircase behind the bar. Chachie got her back there for me. God, those were good times.

My prospecting memories are all from just that, my memory. Once I patched out, I started a log of all the trips I took, so the rest of this, the dates and events will be spot on. Again, as this goes, I may have to change some names to protect the innocent.

Yes, I was married during this time to Lucille. We divorced in 2019 after being legally separated in 2016. Nothing brought to light in this book about my adulterous ways back then are nothing new to Lu. I am an honest person to the point of letting her know everything I ever was doing. She chose to deal with it in her own way. So before you judge me, remember the shit you've done or are doing without your ole lady or ole man knowing. At least I had the balls to tell mine the truth.

I loved going to Orange County. The ride was about two hours, and it was a great ride. Mostly, I liked Orange County 'cause Chaz and I had grown close and Tommy Pipe was such a fuckup I knew no attention would be drawn to me. Ed and I got really close as well. Ed is now in our Moore County, North Carolina, chapter, and I don't get to see him as much as I would like to; but when we get together, it's always a good time. Chaz is now an active member in Bergen, so we get to spend a lot of time together. He has become one of my closest and trusted brothers. Not even your mother loves you more than me, brother!

Wednesday, September 1, 2006, myself, Igor, Kenny, and Phil head to Maryland to RB's house. We were going to rack out there, then the five of us were heading to Oak Grove, Kentucky, chapter for nationals. Well, Wednesday, Thursday, and most of Friday I quickly realized why Bergen was called the "rain chapter." We rode through tropical storm, El Niño, all day Thursday to Lexington, Kentucky. We went to a brother Tony Pignato's (who was at the time retired out of OGKY chapter) house. Tony Pignato and his wife had an unbelievable spread laid out for us. We all got cleaned up and ate and shot the shit. After a while, Tony asked me if I was tired. I said yes. He said his wife would show me to where we were all gonna sleep upstairs to follow her upstairs. Well, now Tony's wife is a very attractive woman, and she had on these really tiny shorts. I'm going up the stairs behind her, and about halfway up, I hear, "PROSPECT!" It was Tony.

"Yes, patch holder," I responded, both of us stopping on the stairs.

"Are you looking at my wife's ass?" he asked.

"Yes, I am, patch holder," I answered.

"Carry on, good man" was all he said, and everyone started cracking up.

I told you I never lie!

The next morning, we all got up early, ate, and saddled up for the last leg of the trip to OGKY. Tony and I ended up following in his truck with a trailer 'cause the Orange guys called and said that prospect Tommy Pipes bike broke down about seventy-five miles from Lexington. It was decided I would ride with Tony and we would get Pipe and then they would drop me off at my bike and I would follow Tony and Pipe in the truck to OGKY.

Tony had me dying in the truck. He does have jokes, and he impersonates RB better then RB. We got Pipe, and we all ended up rolling into OGKY. It was the first time I'd seen CC since he was in Bergen. I had a few introductions, then it was behind the bar. There was a meeting being held, and a brother came to me and asked my name. I told him, and he introduced himself as "Mr. Tugboat from downtown Marvyn, Alabama, Opelika chapter of the Wingmen nation." He handed me a bar card and pointed to this little skinny-looking, meth-head broad who looked to be half his age.

He said, "Prospect, this is my lady. I have to go into a meeting, and you need to keep feeding her drinks. No matter what!" He continued to say, "If the card runs out, run a tab. You have my word, I'm good for it."

I said, "Roger that. I'll take care of it."

He grabbed my hand and said, "Prospect, look at me." I did. He said, "No, look at me how ugly I am. If she doesn't get drunk, I don't get any pussy. Understand?"

I tried really hard not to laugh and insured him I'd take care of it. Tugboat and I got very close over the years. He was a great brother and a great man. God rest Mr. Tugboat from downtown Marvyn, Alabama's soul.

Later that night I met a brother named Cowboy also from the Opelika, Alabama, chapter. He was a very large man, well over six feet, and probably close to, if not over, the three-hundred-pound mark (sloppy weight though).

He came to the bar and ordered a drink. I gave him the drink, and without tasting it, he held it out over the bar and poured it all over my boots. He then said, "Make me another one, prospect. That one tasted like shit."

I made another one and then gave it to him. As he started walking away, I called to him and said, "Patch holder, I'm sorry, what was your name again?"

He turned and looked at me, all cocky, "I'm Cowboy Opelika."

"Roger," I said.

I pulled out my notebook, and Cowboy was now on my short list. My short list was for those who acted like an ass to me and would be dealt with at a later date. More on Cowboy later on.

Later that night I was walking from the meeting building to the clubhouse when I heard the famous cry of *prospect.* I turned around to find another prospect was the one yelling it at me. His name was Railroad from the Long County, Georgia, chapter. When I turned and noticed he was a prospect, he realized the look on my face wasn't a happy one. He immediately apologized and acknowledged his ignorance. We laughed about it, and I helped him get some drinks for the brothers who were playing poker in the meeting room building.

Railroad had it real tough Friday night. He was the dealer for the poker game *all night long.* Railroad and I ended up exchanging numbers, and we have become very close brothers since our first encounter.

Friday blended into Saturday, and I was pulling security detail outside the meeting site in the parking lot. My first real taste of Kentucky heat. About halfway through the meeting, Bucket (a brother from Oak Grove) grabbed me and asked me and two other prospects to go to the barn and help him start barbecuing. The barn was the OGKY chapter's "other" property—a bunch of acres in the middle of nowhere with a big old barn, a large pond, a big field for "biker games," and a shooting range.

Bucket had this fifteen-or-so-foot-long homemade grill set up and was screaming at a prospect who apparently brought the wrong box of utensils to the barn. So we had a box of large serving spoons but no spatulas. I came over and told Bucket I'd take care of it. I grabbed a couple of the spoons and a crescent wrench he used to put the grill together. I found a tree stump and proceeded to hammer the spoons into flat spatulas with the wrench. And the "spoonschela" was created. One of them is on a plaque in the Bergen clubhouse. Bucket had it made for me and gave it to me when I patched out.

I met so many brothers that weekend. Most notably Roy Willy, Phenix City; Bull, Long County; Ranger Rick, OGKY; Mikey Tee, OGKY; DJ North, Georgia; Albie, Fayetteville; OB, OGKY; Weird Al, OGKY; Von Zipper, Savannah; Rico Suave, OGKY; Bucket, OGKY; Patrick, Moore County; August, Moore County; Super Dave, Savannah; Shadow, Savannah; Buzz, Savannah; Humphreys, Fayetteville; Strickland, Fayetteville; and the man, the myth, the legend, Lee Carrillo. CC had brought me over to meet Lee who was sitting at a table. He stood up to shake my hand and was noticeably nursing a bad back. I asked if he was okay and said he had forgotten his pain meds for his back. I reached into my prospect bag and handed him four perks. I think Lee would've patched me right then and there if Bergen would've let him.

Lee, over the years, has become my mentor and father figure in the club. He is who I call for advice or just to vent. I served under him for almost a decade on the national executive counsel as his national SAA and national vice president. I was his choice to pass the national president's seat to when he decided eight years in the seat was enough. I would kill or die for that man without hesitation. I love him and respect him and thank God I got to meet him and get to go through this crazy world with him as a brother. Por vida, brother.

Sunday morning the Bergen chapter and I started our journey back to Dirty Jersey. The good thing about riding in the rain is, most of the time, you get a great weather ride home. We rolled to the bottom end of Virginia and stopped for fuel. The patch holders were all arguing about when and where to stop. Some wanted to stop now; some wanted to roll another hundred or so miles. RB looked at me and asked what I thought.

I told him, "If we roll another seventy or so miles that would put us in Roanoke, Virginia. I know some lady friends there I can call, and I'm sure they would meet up with us and show us around town."

He looked at me like I was full of shit and said, "Okay, Roanoke it is."

We rolled into Roanoke and got a room at a Days Inn. I made a call to a friend of mine, Dani. Dani, Mary, and Kim are three women I had the pleasure of meeting in Myrtle Beach at bike week three years before. We had all kept in touch and met up in Myrtle every year. I told her to round up the girls and meet me at my room later on in the day. Around 1900 hours, there was a knock on the door, and RB, with whom I was sharing the room with, answered. There was a blond, brunette, and a redhead standing there and asked in that beautiful Southern drawl if Joey was there. RB said, "Hooold ooon." He closed the door, kissed me on the forehead, and said, "The only way you aren't going to patch is if you die!" We all went to dinner and then to a local bar/pool hall for the night. We all had a great time.

The next morning, we were in the parking lot, and once again, the patch holders were arguing. This time, Phil was complaining he had to eat, and eat now. RB and Kenny were trying to explain to him that we were on the outer edge of a thunderstorm moving our way, and "let's burn off our fuel tanks then stop to eat." Phil was having none of it.

Finally, RB said, "Okay, you pussy, we will stop to eat."

We headed out of the parking lot and found a McDonald's. Everyone headed inside except for Phil. I stayed with him, and he ordered me inside.

I went in, and we were all getting our food when RB said, "Where is Phil?"

I told him, "He is in the parking lot and told me to go inside."

Apparently, Phil was pissed at RB and didn't want to eat now. RB looked out the window to see Phil sitting on his bike, giving him the finger.

Now RB lost his shit and pulled a plastic knife from the tray and said, "I'm going to cut his fucking throat," as he started for the door.

Little Kenny and Igor grabbed RB and explained that if he did that, we would definitely be caught in the rain after someone called the cops and we were cuffed and arrested for killing Phil. RB calmed down, and we proceeded to finish eating. I don't think Phil ever realized how close he was to being fucked up by RB that day. Doesn't matter. Phil ended up quitting a few years later. The rest of the trip home was uneventful, but great ride home.

That at the time was the longest trip I had ever taken in just a four-day period. It definitely set the hook in me for long trips that test your limits and the bikes limits. I would go on in the future to ride to Devil's Elbow, Missouri, in under sixteen hours, and going to Georgia or Alabama in around twelve to thirteen hours was my norm. I once rode from Delray Beach, Florida, to Dirty Jersey straight through 1,338 miles in eighteen hours forty-five minutes—a personal best.

After the trip to nationals, I experienced my first loss of a brother in the club. Dozer from Orange County was on his way to CC's house from OGKY. He was involved in a wreck and didn't survive his injuries. I remember Bermuda Mike calling me to inform me. It was a big dose of reality as to the dangers we face when traveling on a motorcycle. The following weekend, Orange County would hold a life celebration for Dozer. Brothers came in from all over the country to pay respects to Dozer.

It was when I met Stew from Devil's Elbow, Missouri, though I think he might have been active with North Georgia at that time. I also had the great honor of meeting and starting an unbelievable brotherhood with Wil Williams from our OGKY chapter. Wil was deployed during the national. I spent most of that weekend with Wil, Stew, August, and Patrick.

Earlier in the day, I had to go with Tommy Pipe in his truck to his house and get a grill. I couldn't stand Pipe. He was lazy, dirty, and just the wrong side of the prideful White trash. We pulled up to his home, and it was worse than I was expecting. We pulled around back, and the smell of dog shit was pretty strong (his wife rescued pits). I got out of the truck and was sidestepping shit mines everywhere. Now, I worked in a sewerage treatment plant. Not much can get me to gag. However, the back door opened, and this little human came running out in just a diaper. The diaper was down to its knees and full of molded shit. I am not exaggerating. Then a second little human emerged, a little bigger than the first. The smell coming from that house was like nothing I have ever been exposed to. I have been around rotting bodies, and my work permeates some of the worst smells in the world. I began dry heaving. I looked at Tommy and asked him, "What the fuck is wrong with them?" and "How could they enter that home, nonetheless live in it?" I walked back to the truck and just waited for him to put the grill in the bed of the truck. When he entered the truck, I just said, "Don't say a word and I won't abuse you." I told Chaz they really shouldn't cook on that grill. They didn't.

One of the highlights of that Saturday night was this local woman who was a little on the back nine of life and lived the front nine pretty hard. Well, she decided no one was paying her enough attention. She then proceeded to strip naked and start swinging on the stripper pole. It was one of those situations when you'd rather they kept the clothes on. Anyway, Patrick came out of the head and saw this and said something to the tune of "oh my." She didn't hear the sarcasm. She then bent over and dared him to smack her on the ass. Well, Patrick wound up from Lower Mississippi and sent her face-first into the booth in front of her.

Patrick was walking over to us, arms raised in victory, when we heard, "Is that all you got?" Ole girl was standing tall (trying not to cry) with her hands on her hips.

Well, Wil looked at me and said, "Prospect, give me something to smack her ass with."

Well, I kicked off (I don't tie my laces) my size 12 Timberland steel-toed boot and handed it to him. So Patrick put her in a head-lock, and Wil smacked her *hard* on the ass.

She went to one knee, and then you hear it again, *sniff, sniff,* "Is that all you got?"

Well, let's just say, all I could think of was, *I'm going to have to hide a body and burn my favorite pair of boots 'cause the body has the right prints all over it!*

Now, for those bleeding-heart liberals reading this and any ole ladies that may be taking a peek at this, *she loved it.* She ended up blowing, like, five brothers in the camper out back and then hooked up with a brother from Devil's Elbow. I can't remember his name. I called him Andy Gibb 'cause that's who he looked like. He, like, fell in love and ended up shacking up with her for, like, three weeks till she broke his heart and asked him when he was returning to Missouri. He ended up becoming a quitter some years later. Yep, you guessed it, over a broad.

While I was south of the Mason–Dixon line, Bermuda Mike had asked me to pick up BC powder for him and some for the club-house as well. BC powder is a powder form of aspirin for those who don't know. Back in the day, you couldn't get it north of the line. It is packaged like a dealer with OCD would package cocaine. Nice cellophane folded perfectly, even has its own elastic band to form a nice bundle. Well, I bought a box for myself as well and kept about ten or so packages in my kutte. I was riding with a friend of mine,

Big Bobby (civilian). We were blasting down Route 23 south out on a Sunday ride. I used to wear my beanie helmet with the strap real loose and have the helmet on the back of my neck. Well, I didn't see the cop in time to pull the helmet up. We got lit up and pulled over. Now, my friend Bobby was about six foot four inches and around four hundred pounds, no front teeth, and was a pretty intimidating guy. Cop was young, real young, and visibly very nervous.

I told him, "A no-helmet ticket is equivalent to no-seat belt. Just give me the ticket so we can go."

He went to the car with our papers and was there for over ten minutes when two more cars rolled up.

I looked at Bobby and asked him if he had any warrants. He replied, "Not that I know of."

Young buck came up with his other gang members standing in the back and asked if I would consent to a search. I said, "Absolutely not." He informed me he would have a K9 unit come, and if the dog gives an alert, he would have the right to search anyway. The alert can be anything the cop decides it to be, so there would be an alert for sure. I was thinking, *What the fuck, I don't have anything to hide, so fuck you. Go for it.* They found nothing on my bike at all and then asked me to empty all my pockets. I stuck my hand inside my kutte and grabbed the BC powder packages, and the light bulb went off in my head! I was going to have some fun with this asshole. I pulled my hand out and closed it around the packages like I didn't want him to see them.

He grabbed them, and a big smile came across his face. He asked me, "What are these?"

I replied, "I want to call my lawyer!"

He cuffed me and sat me on the curb, and they told Bobby to take off. He went about two hundred yards down the shoulder and pulled over to wait and watch. This is pre-smartphone days, folks. No body cameras, so cops used to get away with a lot of shit. So back to Officer Barney. I had a feeling the older cop observing knew what was going on and what I was up to. Officer Barney went and got the test kit from his car, and he just couldn't keep the smile off his face. He opened a package and put some in a capsule, added some chemical, and shook it up. He was excited, expecting the liquid to turn bright blue, and nothing. Took another package and repeated process with same result. Finally, on, like, the fourth one, older officer came over, stood me up, and uncuffed me. Barney looked and asked what he was doing.

He looked at me and said, "Get out of here." I smiled, and he said, "Well played."

Now Barney was losing his shit. Old officer looked and said, "Rookie, it's aspirin. Clean it up and get out of here!" I would later find out that word in the cop shops was, I was a gunrunner and was usually armed. Lies!

October 20, 2006. We rolled to Orange for a tri-county meeting. Well, the meeting was, they patched Ed and Tommy Pipe. I was super proud and happy for Ed. He worked and earned every bit of his eagle. Tommy I still don't get how he got votes, but "it is what it is." The night was theirs, and everyone partied and showed them Wingmen love.

The weekend of October 27, 2006, brother CC was flying in to hang out with the Bergen brothers. He and I were planning on a trip into the city to go to the World Trade Center site. CC is a Savanna fireman and wanted to pay his respects to the September 11 memorial.

The next night, we all went to Rockland's clubhouse, and CC presented me with my MCs. Later that night I was behind the bar, and the place was pretty crowded. Tommy Pipe was sitting at the bar next to Big Willie and was dangling a cigarette from his lips. We all know what the lighter is for and what to do and not to do with it.

I said to Tommy, "I see you, Tommy, li'l busy over here." To no avail, he continued to dangle the cigarette. I finally walked over and lit it for him. He then reached out and grabbed my right hand with both his and tried to take my lighter. I laughed and said, "What the fuck, Tommy, really?"

Now he had a foot on the bar, trying to get this from my hand. Well, Big Willie sees what's going on and says to Tommy "what the fuck are you stupid" and backhands Tommy. Tommy let go and proceeded to fall to the floor. That's how Tommy Pipe made the short list.

Chaz talked CC and I into going and staying at his house. Never—and I mean ever—get into a cage with Nighttime Chaz. I have seen some shit in my day, and I really thought for sure we were going to die. Now Chaz had always been saying his ex-wife, Rachel, took everything when she left. I figured he was exaggerating a bit and never paid it any mind. Well, when we walked into his house, he wasn't exaggerating. I mean, the only thing in the place was his queen-size bed, two single-size beds, a recliner, and a TV on a box. No stove, refrigerator, microwave, dinette set, couch, utensils, plates, nothing. It was pretty amazing to witness. The next morning, I went to get my MCs sewn on. There was a Spanish woman up the road from Chaz's house he told me to go to. I showed her what I needed, and she said to leave it. I told her that was not an option. She then said, "Okay, I'll do it now." She had an extremely thick Spanish accent. I asked her how much, and I heard, "Twenty-eight dollars." A li'l pricey, but I agreed. Twenty minutes later, I put them on and checked them out in the mirror.

"Looks great," I said. I threw thirty-five dollars on the counter.

She looked at me and said, "Where's the rest?"

I looked at her like, *What the fuck?*

She then loudly and slowly said, "I SAID EIGHTY DOLLARS."

I laughed and told her, for eighty, it better come with a blow job. I told her to call the cops, I'll be up the street. Fucking immigrants.

I was in the home stretch now. Top, bottom, and MCs, I was hitting my marks and kept my shot group tight. I wasn't going to let myself get lazy, thinking I could slack off. The month of November was uneventful.

Friday, December 1, 2006. Bergen was hosting a tri-county meeting. Little Kenny was my sponsor, and he was stoned as usual. He came up to me and said, "Give me your rags and go get a case of Budweiser cans at the liquor store." I told him he wasn't getting my rags, and we didn't sell Bud in cans, and he should lay off the weed a li'l bit. He didn't know what to say. He kept on me to give him my rags. Finally, Darren came over and said, "Just give them to me." I figured what was going on due to the tri-county meeting, and also Bermuda Mike was leaving for Bermuda in a couple days. I gave them to Darren then went to Kenny and got his car keys. I told him I needed his car to get the beer. He was so stoned he gave them to me. So, yes, I got my beer in a cage!

That night I became a Wingmen. My life as I knew it would change rapidly and dramatically over the next years. I was full of pride and overwhelmed with the gifts and the conversations I had with most of the brothers from Bergen, Rockland, and Orange counties. I also needed to talk to Tommy Pipe. Tommy had a gift for me. I told him to follow me back into the meeting room where it was "quieter." I closed the door behind us, and when he went to hug me, I stiff armed him and told him he needed to defend himself. He was dumbfounded, that is, until my right elbow found the side of his face. He was out for about thirty seconds, and then I told him why I did it. Then I told him I really had nothing for him except for his eagle on his back, and it would be best if we didn't talk unless it was warranted. Then I thanked him for the knife he gave me as a gift.

Over the next few months, I let up a little but dug my spurs in him whenever the situation called for it. Tommy ended up a quitter around a year or so after I patched.

That night we partied, and my now ex-wife was singing the words to a song that was playing on the stereo in the clubhouse. It was "No time" by The Guess Who. She exaggerated the line, "I found myself some wings." She knew me and knew I was diving into the deep end and would give every ounce of me to this new endeavor. She was right.

CHAPTER 7

Active Patch Holder: Year One

The next night, Rockland was having a party. It was cold, but Little Kenny and I rode. My first ride with my eagle, and I'm glad it was with Kenny 'cause, as a prospect, Kenny and I rode the most side by side. I remember just sitting on the couch with Curtis that night, just shooting the shit. It was long, hard road prospecting back then. I didn't spend all my time behind the bar, mixing drinks. We went out to bars, parties, other clubs, and other chapters. I had a great time prospecting. I was able to not have an answer or opinion. All that changed when I became a patch holder. Now I was responsible for my words and actions. Time to earn my eagle every day!

December 16, 2006. I boarded a plane and headed to Savannah. I was met at the airport by Country, Doc Kip, and Von Zipper. They had a leather jacket, a helmet, and Countries Old Yeller bike. I rode with Kip and Zipper to the old Savannah clubhouse. There I met a bunch of brothers while a naked chick was dancing on the pool table. Super Dave had gotten her to come down for me. Yes, I banged her. That was the day I met Robbie "Buckshot" Goodman! This was before he was saved and became a minister. Robbie and I have since had some pretty good conversations and became very close throughout the years. He was one of only two brothers I called during my eight-day hiatus trip to California and back. It was a very spiritual, moving trip for me, and I called Robbie and Mike Roy to share some of my emotions with. More on that when we get to 2019. Love and respect you, brother Buckshot.

We all rode down to Long County. The reason for my trip was, Long County was patching Railroad that evening. I wouldn't have missed it for the world. I had to stay out of sight because he would've figured it out if he saw me. So Zipper (a man of many women) called an acquaintance of his and took me to her "trailer." I spent a few hours there waiting for the all-clear call.

Around 1900 hours, I got the call and headed on over. That night was great. Railroad really appreciated me making the trip. That was the night I met his now wife, Leslie. Now this was back when I could drink like a mick. I remember CC, PD, and I standing around a table around 0400 hours, none of us wanting the be the next to tap out (there were bodies everywhere). Finally, CC said, "If we all go down together, we are all the last ones standing." Man, I hit the couch and was out in, like, thirty seconds.

That weekend showed me the right way to treat a brother who is traveling into your AO for a special reason other than a scheduled party or run. I had a bike, I had women, and I wasn't allowed to take a dime out of my pocket. I got to meet a bunch of brothers I haven't before and had an awesome time. Most of all, I was there for my brother Railroad's big night. Love you, brother, beginning to the wall together.

January 5, 2007. The Bergen chapter decided by a vote to elect me the chapter's treasurer. I was a bookie for a bunch of years for my uncles, so should be a no-issue thing.

January 12, 2007. Myself, Ronnie, Kenny, and Igor flew into Atlanta for January nationals in Opelika. I know what you're all thinking: two trips, two airplanes. It was a particularly bad winter in New Jersey that year, and riding out of the state and/or back into it was just not going to happen.

We rented a car in Atlanta, and we met Jack Baker at a Cracker Barrel on the way down from the airport for lunch. Jack was active in our North Georgia chapter at the time and already a legend in the club. The "Baker Boys" consisted of Jack and his brothers, Slick, Charlie, and Indio (Ivan). All put in serious work back in the day for this club, and all are straight-up 100 percent Wingmen. It was the beginning of a very great friendship and brotherhood between Jack and I. We to this day talk at least once a week. I've been to Texas to visit him and his family (his mom makes the best tamales, hands down!). Love you, you little angry Mexican.

When we arrived at the clubhouse, RB was hammered, I mean sideways fucked up. All he kept saying was, "I should've eaten." That night I got a lot of face time with Lee Carrillo. I hadn't seen him since the national in OGKY when I was a prospect. I received a bunch of gifts that night from brothers and got to meet a bunch more. The next morning, I sat in on my first national meeting.

That night RB was sober, and he wanted to introduce me to brother David Tope. Tope was a legend, and there were many different stories surrounding David. The biggest being, he won't even acknowledge you if you don't have five stars on your year bar (five active years in the club). Well, RB takes me out front, and David is sitting on a bench. He introduces me to Tope and walks away. I'm sure it was because RB brought me over and introduced us that David gave me the time of day, but I ended up on that bench with him and Scar in conversation for a few hours. I learned a lot and was definitely envied by a lot of the younger patch holders who were shunned by David for conversation.

David was deployed a lot over the years. I remember being in his garage one summer when he was home talking about bikes and brotherhood with a prospect named Dustin Hart. Dustin would patch and become one of the most solid brothers in this club, and one of my favorites as well. David and I have had our disagreements over the years. One thing, I always learned from David. And I have to say, as I grew older in the club, I understand a lot of his ways and thought process a lot better.

March 2, 2007. Barry from Bergen and I decided to jump in his truck and head to Fayetteville for the weekend, just to get away. That weekend I met the man, the myth, the legend, Mr. Patrick Murphy himself. Murph was the guy who started the club while deployed in Verona, Italy, back in the spring of 1976. The club was called the Freedom Riders MC back then. We would later retire that chapter due to brothers rotating back to the States. The club was growing in Vicenza, Italy, and in 1979 we would become the Wingmen Motorcycle Club.

I spent as much time as I could with Murph, and he gave a great history lesson on the club. Then he gave me some great advice. He was in the tail end of writing his book. He told me the hardest part was remembering all the dates and runs and names of people that influenced him throughout the years. Then he said, "Keep a log of everything you do, where you go, and with whom." Well, I did. I have every mile and trip I rode since my patch date. Thank you, Murph. It is going to make this endeavor a lot easier. Love you, brother.

April 7, 2007. The chapter attended a BBQ hosted by a national LEO (law enforcement officer) MC. I know, I know, a cop club, but we all ended up getting PBA cards from their members. Good trade-off. The only reason I bring this event up is, I met "Big Red" at this event. We became close friends, and I would later introduce her to my brother Ditch, who was in our Phenix City chapter at the time. They would go on to marry and have a family together. They are two of the best people to know, and I am blessed to have them in my life. More about all that later. Love you two.

Now, let me give my *opinion* of LEO clubs. Never understood the concept. You spend your working hours harassing most clubs and bikers in general, then you all dress up like us on the weekends and play biker. You get drugs from the dealers you "let deal" and then bust people who buy from the same dealers. I am speaking from definitive knowledge of said actions. I have seen it with my own eyes, so fuck you if you think I am lying or shitting you and yours.

You drive drunk and then arrest others for the same offense. If you get in an accident while driving drunk, you have another of your "gang" cover your shit. It's cool, I would do the same for any of my brothers or close friends. I just won't put on cop clothes and pretend I'm a cop during the week.

And biggest of all, when you get confronted and about to eat an elbow, I always hear, "But I'm a cop!" Sorry, my elbow doesn't discriminate. I have fought many cops and always get that line, like it makes a difference at that moment. Talk like a man, then you can catch hands like a man for your words.

When a member of a LEO club asks me how long I have been riding, I tell them, "Back when cops didn't want to be me."

Now, I have a few civilian friends who are cops or were cops. One I grew up with and consider my family, Dave Norris. I remember posting up on the roof of his home with a rifle, ready to kill for his family when they first moved into Wallington and were the first Black family there. They got death threats and had crosses burned on their lawn. His father cosigned my first car loan for me, and I call his parents Mom and Dad.

We did some stupid shit together growing up, and the only reason he became a cop is, he is Black, and Wallington, New Jersey, needed a Black on the force! Yes, Dave, you know it's true, so shut up. There is no way a White guy was getting that job with the same driving and arrest record! Dave and I spent more time in the back of a cop car together than he has driving one for the last twenty-five or so years. I love you and your family, Dave. You made my teen and early twenties memorable, and we achieved godlike status in our circle. Man, Dave, the shit we did.

The other is a guy by the name of Bobby Ossig. He is a retired PO. Bobby is straight-up, legit great civilian I call my brother. I know, push comes to shove, Bobby would have my back, no questions asked, and he knows I'd have his. Love you, Bobby.

So LEO clubs. I, me, my opinion is, pick a side. Don't wear the uniform of two different "gangs" and live two different lifestyles at once. You're all in my world, or you're not in my world.

April 19, 2007. We had a prospect, "George," in Bergen. He worked with me and hung around then stood up. He and I rode down to Long County for the pimp and hoe ball. Man, it fucking rained all the way there. We had a great time, and it was when I met someone who would become one of my best friends, Aimee Wilson. She was dating a brother from our new Calhoun County chapter, Ron Harris. Aimee and I just hit it off and became great friends. We would end up being there for each other through some of our most trying times in our lives.

Her daughter, Taylor, was diagnosed with leukemia and continues to fight the effects of it to this day. We were there for each other through her daughter's battle and Heather's battle with cancer.

Now this is a lesson of always listen to your gut. Some of us were playing poker. A bunch of local girls walked into the party on Friday night. Usually, it's brothers only and a few invited guests on the Friday night of a big event. But who is going to kick out five broads walking in? There were a few civilian guys there that were invited by a brother as well. Well, one of them, a cute, pale-white blond, walked right over to me and introduced herself and literally asked me to take her into the bunk room. CC was sitting next to me, and I remember the look on his face when I told her I was playing cards with my brothers, maybe later. Well, she walked over to another brother who was at the bar, and he accepted the offer. She was on a mission for sure. CC looked at me and asked me why I turned that down. I just told him there was something off in my gut telling me to pass on it.

Well, about thirty minutes later, Pale Girl came out of the bunk room, hair a mess, and went into the lady's room with one of her friends. Then the friend came out and came up to CC and said, "C, we have a problem. I think your brother just raped my friend!" As upset as I was with the allegation to my brother, I couldn't pat myself on the back hard enough for my decision. There was no way he raped her; it was obvious she was a psycho. So the friend called the cops. Now, I am from New Jersey. I expected helicopters, SWAT swinging in through the windows with ropes, and myself and all my brothers in cuffs. Man, the South is really different from the north. Three officers showed up at the clubhouse. One took Pale Girl on the front porch. One took our brother out back. One was just standing inside, not saying a word. None of them asked to turn off the music. None asked anyone to stop drinking, dancing, playing pool; hell, they didn't even ask anyone not to leave! CC and I followed first officer out the front with Pale Girl.

He looked right at her and in a very thick Georgia accent asked her, "You the gal that got raped?"

She was trying to cry and said yes. He literally pulled her collar from her neck and then lifted her shirt and scanned her body, spun her around a few times, and said, "Don't look like you got raped. Why don't you tell me what really happened."

I was thinking, *This chick is going to lose her shit, and this guy is going to get fired, and she is going to sue the city.* Pale Girl just said nothing. So they packed her up and our brother, and they went to the station. An hour or so later, we got the word she confessed to not being raped and to having consensual sex with our brother 'cause her ex-boyfriend was there (one of the guys playing pool) and she wanted to make him jealous. She decided, when he didn't come busting in the bunk room to stop her from fucking a brother, she would go the rape route, hoping to get him to sympathize for her. Fucking lunatics in this world. Always listen to your gut! I avoided being in the middle of that shit by doing so.

May 6, 2007. Bergen attended a tri-county meeting in Orange along with Rockland. There was a lot of MC movement going on in New York and New Jersey. Joe Dwyer "JD" was there and attended our meeting. He was in our Fayetteville chapter at the time. I remember one specific thing he said, and it has stuck with me since, and I apply it in every situation I come across when dealing with anyone. "Passiveness breeds aggression." No truer words were ever spoken. I carry those words with me into every meeting with another club. Never take a step back, or you will be run through.

May 23, 2007. Myself, Chaz, and a prospect from Devil's Elbow by the name of Schott headed to Fayetteville. This was the starting point of a really bad week of drinking, riding, sex, and bad decisions. We got to Fayetteville and kicked it into high gear. That night I drank, a lot. I woke up at, like, 0530 in a house I didn't recognize next to a naked woman on the floor (whom I also didn't recognize). I found my kutte on the floor under the love seat I was half on, half off and called brother Ian from my cell phone. He was our national SAA at the time.

He answered and said, "This better be important at this hour, Butta."

I told him I didn't know where I was. He asked where I went to after the bar.

I asked him, "What bar?" I didn't remember leaving the clubhouse! I told him to hold on, and I grabbed the naked broad by the hair and asked, "Hey, hey, chick, do you know where we are?"

She replied, "My name is Rosie [not her real name], and no, I don't know. You brought me here on your bike."

"Fuck," I told Ian. "She doesn't know either."

Just then I heard a door open and close and heard footsteps coming down the hall. I thought, *Great, I gotta fight naked.* Well, lo and behold, it was brother Ricky two from Fayetteville in his BDUs going to work.

"Butta, my casa you casa," he said, laughing, seeing the confusion and sudden concern in my face. He walked out the front door.

I told Ian, "I'm at Ricky's house." I told him the broad was hot, so I'd call him back for directions in a few.

From Fayetteville, I rode to see a great civilian friend of mine. His house was in Kernersville, North Carolina. His name is James. He and I met in Myrtle Beach during bike week back in 1996. He is someone I call brother and family. I would kill or die for him and his family. James is clean and sober, so it was a good idea to be with him for a few days before the national weekend.

James and I, along with about twenty or so others from around the country and Canada, met every year in Myrtle Beach for bike week from 1996 till 2007. We had some crazy times, maybe worth a whole other book in the future.

I want to tell one story though because it is fucking hilarious and a good reason not to do illegal drugs. James and I were at the Rat Hole. I was hammered, and then I decided to take mushrooms. Well, the night was going great I hooked up with a hottie from West Virginia, and she jumped on the back of my bike at closing time, and the three of us were heading for the hotel. Well, those that know Myrtle Beach know the Rat Hole and the long-ass road that goes through the military installation back toward town. Well, safe to say, at 0300 hours, it was desolate.

All was well till I started seeing purple waves replacing the road and what looked like green and red lightning and shit. I was 100 percent straight-up tripping. I pulled over and got off my bike and just laid down in the grass to enjoy. James knows me and knows I'm good, just won't ride till I'm able to again. Well, ole girl is getting impatient, and I tell her to walk back or get a ride. Not two minutes later, a few bikes came by and stopped to see if we were okay. I told them to take her with them.

James and I were just chilling in the grass for about an hour or so, and I said, "I'm pretty good, I think. Let's go." We saddled up and were just getting into town when James started choking and grabbing his mouth and pointing for me to pull over.

Now, I was still tripping, and I thought I saw smoke coming from his mouth while he was trying to shout to pull over. I was like, *Damn, how long is this shit going to last?* Then I thought, *I need to find the guy I got them from and get more before we leave Myrtle!*

We finally pulled over, and James was, no shit, choking. I thought I was going to have to do the Heimlich maneuver or some shit. I looked at him, and I saw there was something protruding from his mouth, and it was moving, and there was definitely smoke coming out of his mouth!

James finally got a hold of it and pulled it out of his throat. It was a fucking moth the size of a small bird! When he would cough or breathe out, the dust shit that is on their wings was coming out of his mouth like smoke! Always keep your mouth closed when riding.

James was gasping for air and glad to be breathing, and I was on the fucking ground, laughing so hard I thought I was going to pass out. Just when you think you've seen it all! Okay, back to the original trip.

James and I rolled into the old fairgrounds in Moore County Friday afternoon. I met Walter from Fayetteville. He was prospecting at the time and was in charge at the gate. We were having a great time hanging at the bar in the barn with Ian, Frankie the Elbow, CC, Jack Baker, Ron Harris, and a few others when a woman came up to me and asked if I was "Butta from Bergen County."

I answered, "Why, yes, I am."

She then asked me if I had a room and if I would take her to it.

CC just looked at me and said, "You know it's that Puerto Rican-looking mustache that you have is why these chicks like you?"

I said, "Whatever works," and put her on the back of my bike and went back to my room.

Now, this is where shit gets weird. I was banging her out, putting on a show, and she started saying, "Butta, Butta," over and over. Me being so vain and all, I thought, *Yeah, I got this one in the stable for whenever I want it now.*

Well then, she said, "You have to stop. I'm having a sugar attack!"

I jumped up, and was like, "What?"

"I'm diabetic and am having a sugar attack. I need something with sugar in it."

I threw on my boxers and ran across the street into this gas station and slid to a stop like Tom Cruise in that silly movie. I looked at the very large Black woman behind the counter and told her I needed a honey bun and a coke! She looked at me all wide-eyed and just pointed in the direction and said, "Da honey buns is over dare!" Then it hit me. I was standing in a gas station in my wet-in-the-front boxers with a half a hard-on, asking where the honey buns were (fucking alcohol). I grabbed two honey buns and a bottle of coke and swore I would return to pay in a bit. I then ran out and got back to the room. She (again, I'll change the name; you will see in a minute why. I'll call her Sue) started eating and drinking the items. I waited and finally asked if she was feeling better. She said yes. I threw her back on the bed, went into rabbit mode, busted a nut, and told her to get dressed and get out. That was way too much drama for me, and now I was sober again.

So I ended up back at the bar, drinking, so I had an excuse to make more bad decisions. Well, Rosie from the other night texted me to tell me she would be there in a while. At around 1900 hours or so, I saw Rosie walking toward the bar in my direction.

CC hit me in the arm and said, "Hey, isn't that diabetic chick over there?"

I turned to see Sue coming from the other direction, and she was heading right at Rosie. Well, they converged pretty much right in front of CC and I.

"Hello, Rosie."

"Hello, Sue."

"Just so you know, I fucked Butta before," said Sue.

Rosie looked at me and said, "Why would you do that? You knew I was coming."

My reply was, "Well, that was this afternoon. Now it's nighttime." Didn't go over quite as well as I thought it would. She scampered off, all pissed off. I then looked at Sue and said, "You know her and knew she and I hooked up the other night, didn't you?"

She winked, kissed my cheek, and said, "I can't stand that bitch."

She fucked me to get back at an old friend. Women.

The rest of the night was spent partying with my brothers. We had a blast. That was the last national at the old fairgrounds. The next morning, we had our national meeting, and I received my first service award from Bergen County.

A few months later, Bernie from Devil's Elbow and his wife came to Bergen and stayed at my house. We were in my basement, playing cards, and he handed me a brown paper bag that said "Butta's survival kit." I opened it, and inside was a can of Coke, twenty-four-hour energy drink, a honey bun, and a condom. I still have it to this day.

June 1, 2007. The Bergen chapter decided by a vote that I would be elected to be their vice president. I was honored and ready for the challenge.

June 14, 2007. I rode down to CC's house to attend Long County's anniversary party. CC and I rode to Effingham County, which was a big steel hanger in Grip's backyard. I had decided that I wanted to ride my motorcycle to every clubhouse my first year. So, with this, I could check off Effingham. Long County had a killer party. I got to meet Mr. Socko (thanks, DJ), something I could've lived with never experiencing. A bunch of us hammered out some broad named Melissa. Funny thing, myself and Stevo had to stop some locals from stealing her. She was passed out on the front lawn.

We waited till they had the door of their truck open before asking what they were doing. They were trying to say they knew her and were taking her home. I asked where she lived and knew they were lying because I knew she lived in a motel room across the bridge. We told them it would be best if they put her back on the grass where they found her.

July 12, 2007. This next trip is a very special trip for me. Curtis from Rockland, due to his illness, didn't get to ride out of state anymore. He was talking to me a few weeks before at a Bergen open house how he wanted to go to Opelika's anniversary party. I told him I would love to go with him, and the plans were set.

Brain let Curtis use his new Street Glide. And off we went. We made it to Opelika in two days, settled in, and had a great time Friday night. Calhoun County was a probate chapter and just secured an awesome clubhouse in Anniston, Alabama, on Tenth St. Curtis knew if we rode there Saturday morning, we could claim first brothers from up north to visit. So it was a plan we would ride to Anniston in the morning.

Saturday morning we saddled up. I have to say, I never, never wear shorts on a bike. Well, that morning I wore shorts. It was around 140 miles, I think, up to Anniston. We took a two-lane highway 431 north, and it was awesome. We rode into Anniston, found the clubhouse, and boom, no one was around. Go figure. They were all either in Opelika or on the way there, I would suppose.

Now this is where the trip gets interesting. I told you about the shorts for a reason. On the way back, it started pouring. I mean straight-up biblical storm. Now, as if that wasn't enough, enter *hail!* Yeah, we couldn't see getting pummeled by golf-ball-size hail. It was bad. I saw a driveway, and we rolled in. It was a small trailer park. The newest trailer looked to be about twenty years old. Everyone was looking out of their windows then, pulling the shades. Well, Curtis lost his shit and started screaming, "We can see you, you fucking pricks! You can't even offer us your porch?"

Now, I'm like, "Curt, these motherfuckers got guns and shit. You need to cut that out, brother." Curtis didn't care. He was hot, and I said, *Fuck it, let him have at it.* Luckily, no one shot us. The storm blew over, and like two wet dogs, we got on the bikes and rolled back into Opelika.

Curtis and I had a great ride back. We rode to the Winchester, Virginia, exit on Route 81 Sunday and finished the ride on Monday. We rode 2,389 miles that weekend. It ended up being the last out-of-state run Curtis would take. I am honored I was able to do that trip with him. Love and miss you, Curtis. "FLESRUOY KCUF OG."

August 16, 2007. I headed to Oak Grove chapter for the annual pistol shoot. I remember this trip for a few reasons very well. First one being, it fucking poured on me from the moment I left my home till Lexington. I stopped at a Pilot gas station. I grabbed some dry clothes and headed into the head. I proceed to put newspaper on the floor by the sink and stripped down naked and started drying off with paper towels.

Just then this big (like six feet, two inches), pretty fat guy with a flannel shirt and a big old cowboy hat on walked in and looked at me and said, "Well, hey there!"

I looked at him and said, "Great, all I need now—gay trucker love."

He responded with, "Oh no, I ain't no trucker."

Brothers, I lost my shit. Thank God I didn't carry back then. I would've gotten twenty to life. I pulled my knife from my kutte and told him to get the fuck out of the room and not think of coming back in till he saw me exit the building. He ran out. Just as I was getting dressed, I heard someone trying not to laugh in a stall. I guess he was in there, dumping out, and I didn't realize he was there. I then screamed at him not to leave the stall till he heard me leave. He was belly laughing by now. The shit you see and hear in a roadside men's room.

I make it to OGKY and meet up with CC. We hit the hotel and then headed over to the clubhouse. The next morning, we all converged on the barn. That was the chapter's property in the middle of nowhere. It had a big barn that had a bar and a stage for entertainment, a nice-sized pond, a big open field for biker games, and a big outdoor shooting range.

They had some good old-fashioned biker games going on: slow ride, find the potato (for the ladies), keg race, and the good old barrel races. Now CC was hammered, I mean slurring drunk. He was looking for someone to lend him a bike to ride in the barrel race. He rode Country's new bagger to the event and didn't want to have a go at it on that.

I remember him trying to get Ditch's new, used soft tail from him. Ditch was hanging on for dear life. A bunch of us were hanging off to the side, watching the races, when all of a sudden, someone screamed, "LOOK OUT!" We turned to see C on my Heritage barreling for the crowd. He slid right next to me and almost dropped her and said, slurring, "You should've locked her." He dropped the clutch and proceeded to gain speed, heading for the first barrel. He didn't even attempt to turn, just sideswiped it, and then very eloquently—and I must say pretty damn gracefully—got off (while she was still going) and headed back to the bar. Best was, it was only, like, 1400 hours. We still had a long way to go!

Later that afternoon, I had my opportunity to have a chat with Cowboy from Opelika. I ran into him behind the barn. I was coming from the port-a-john he was going, and we were alone. He was walking past and said hey. I asked him to come over by me. When he did, I reminded him of what a dick he was to me when I was a prospect. I told him he needed to defend himself, and he literally almost started crying! Running on about how he had a bad heart and couldn't fight and he was sorry, he was drunk, etc. I was so shocked at how big a pussy he was I just walked away. He ended up either quitting or getting thrown out some years later, then he died of a heart attack, I had heard.

August 23, 2007. I got a call from Tommy Turmoil that a brother was in town. I think he said he was helping family move. Anyway, he told me to get to the Rockland clubhouse if I could to meet brother Bossman from Devil's Elbow. I got up there and got to meet Boss. He was one of the charter members of not only Devil's Elbow but our now retired Mannheim, Germany, chapter. I got to sit and have a few beers and hear a lot of the club's history that night.

September 27, 2007. I headed out to Devil's Elbow. Planned on meeting CC, Railroad, and PD in Illinois for some gambling before hitting the clubhouse and the party. CC and them had to cage it for some reason, and I'm glad they did. The picture of me riding with the "Gateway Arch" around me was taken that day by my brother Railroad. One of my favorite pictures.

I got to the casino first. We didn't make reservations, so I was to secure us rooms. I went in, and nothing; they had no rooms available. I came out and was standing by my bike and called C.

I was telling him we had to find a new place, they didn't have any rooms, when this very hot and a little drunk broad in a little black dress on said, "Hey there, hot biker. Do you need a room?"

I told C I'd call him back. She was with another broad and some soft-looking guy.

I said, "Well, yes, I do. I'm meeting some of my brothers here, and they said inside they don't have any rooms."

She said, "I'll make you a deal. If I get you a room, can me and my girl here take pictures on your bike?"

I said, "Of course, you can."

She grabbed my hand. We went inside. She then walked me behind the front desk and got behind the computer. She then summoned one of the workers over and asked if these people had checked in yet while pointing at the screen.

The girl said, "No, they haven't."

She then said, "Hey, biker, what's your name?"

I give her my information, and she handed me two card keys to a three-bedroom suite!

I went to give her my credit card, and she said, "Don't worry. Let's go take those pictures!" She was a manager at the hotel. What luck I got.

Now her and her girlfriend were all over my bike, and the soft guy was snapping pictures. She then wanted to straddle me while I was sitting on the bike for some more shots. She was getting very handsy and really going for broke. Mind you, this was right by the front doors of the hotel/casino, so it was drawing a crowd. Her and her girlfriend were going through the pictures on the camera, and the guy came up and thanked me. He told me they were engaged, but she has a thing for bikers and motorcycles. He shook my hand, the broads gave me a hug, and that was that.

I called CC and told him we were good, we got a suite. He said, "Bro, how much is that going to cost?"

I told him, "Don't worry, I got it."

We went to the casino and got our rooms and then hit the casino floor. We all had no luck; CC, PD, and I played a bank of slots that supposedly had a 97.3 percent chance of winning. Well, I guess CC, PD, and I are the 2.7 percenters of the gambling world. We were supposed to get 2.7 percent tattoos but still haven't gotten them as of yet. And relax not in a diamond.

We rolled into Devil's Elbow and had a great time that day. That night we all went to a local strip club. Brother Elwood and I ended up leaving later than all the others, and we scored a couple of strippers. I remember it got cold, real cold. We were riding around and riding around when we came to a Stop sign, and I asked him if he had any intention of getting us back to the clubhouse. He laughed and said he thought I knew how to get there. One of the half-frozen strippers guided us to the clubhouse.

The next morning, a bunch of us went down to the river for the annual canoe race. CC and I partnered up, and so did Lee and Elwood. Well, we were pretty far in front, and I noticed that Lee and Elwood had been slapping their oars at something in or on the water. Then they started to really get into the rowing, and I had a feeling something was up.

I looked at C and said, "Let's get to the line first and on shore."

We got to the finish line and got our canoe out of the water just as Lee and Elwood were pulling in. They got out of their canoe, and Lee asked me to help with their cooler. I was suspicious. I asked if there was a snake in the cooler. Lee laughed and said no. I asked again, a little slower this time.

"Lee, is there a snake in that cooler?"

He said, "*No*,"—very slowly—"there isn't. On my patch, there is no snake in the cooler."

Well, he wasn't lying because the fucking snake was under the cooler! When I picked it up, it looked to me to be ten feet long. I fell back, catching the contents of the cooler all over my chest and face, and yes, I screamed like a little girl! I fucking hate snakes.

Later that night, a brother came to me and pointed out this very pretty woman. He told me she was his mistress, and he forgot to tell her his wife would be attending the party. She was mad, and he asked me to talk to her, and if I wanted to spend the night with her, I could. He told me he asked her to pick a brother to keep her company, and she picked me. I went over, introduced myself, and she was one of the smartest people I had ever talked to. World politics, bikes, sports, you name it, she had an intelligent conversation for you.

Before I knew it, it was late, around 2200 hours. Now, I had an eleven-hundred-mile trip the next day. I said my goodbyes and headed back to the room. CC and PD were already there. I got down to my boxers and got in bed. Then there was a knock at the door. It was this brother's mistress again, and she asked for me. CC just looked at me and said, "I can't believe this always happens to you." She asked if I would go back to her room for a proper goodbye and send-off.

I followed her a couple doors down and went inside. She then pushed me on the bed, and as she was undressing, she told me she was very angry at my brother and that I needed to just lie there and let her get her anger out, then I could do whatever I wanted. I'm like, "Yeah, of course," all excited, thinking, *Damn, I don't even have to work for it.* Well then, the devil appeared in this little adorable woman. She got on top of me and beat the living shit out of me while having sex with me at the same time. I was frozen in fear and just took it. She scratched me, smacked me, pulled my hair, bit me—pretty sure she was chanting in tongues—then she came and collapsed on top of me. She looked at me and said, "Now you can do whatever you want to me." I went into rabbit mode, busted a nut, and then got the fuck out of there. I got back to my room and looked like I got in a fight with two cats in a potato sack. I had to stop CC from going to her room and shooting her. I tended to my wounds and tried to get some sleep.

November 10, 2007. Attended Chaz's wedding. He was marrying his ex-wife for the second time. Yes, he really did. She was a looker and just as crazy as she was good-looking. But I supported my brother. She would soon become, or as some say was already, pregnant with twins. At least he got two awesome sons out of the ordeal since the marriage failed again. Love you, Chaz, and you know it!

This concludes the notable runs I did my first year as a patch holder. We use a fiscal year that starts and ends November 30. It allows chapters time to pick a candidate for our national Captain Wingmen award. Get all the miles and runs counted up and into the national secretary as to have the award ready to go at the January national. So you will see the years start December 1 for each chapter to follow.

I ended the year with 17,495 club miles. I rode my motorcycle to every Wingmen clubhouse and attended ten run scheduled events. That effort awarded me my first Captain Wingmen award at the January national in 2008.

CHAPTER 8

Year Two

I usually try to set yearly riding goals. 2007 I set a goal to ride to every clubhouse. For 2008 I decided I was going to ride over twenty thousand miles with my eagle on my back.

January 4, 2008. The Bergen chapter decided by a vote to elect me their president. I was up for the challenge and looking forward to representing Bergen to the nation and other clubs.

January 18, 2008. I rode to winter nationals. The weather was cold, but there wasn't any precipitation. I had just bought my first set of heated gear. Money well spent. I had won Captain Wingmen for 2007, and life was good. I had a friend of mine from Daytona meet me at nationals. Her name was Kelli (her real name). She was a great friend. I had visited her many times, and she would meet me in either Long County or Savannah when she could. She found out in early 2015 she had cancer. She passed April 17 that year. She was a great person with a huge heart and someone I had great respect and love for. We had many great times together. I promised her I would speak her name in my prayers every night, and I do, every night. Love and miss you, Miss Kelli.

February 8, 2008. I headed to Daytona to hang out with Kelli. Rode straight through to Daytona and made it in fourteen hours. That weekend I met a member of the Warlocks MC by the name of Lucky. He owned a tattoo shop in town and was dating Kelli's daughter, Ashley (Miss Smasher). We had a great time, and I was treated with great respect by Lucky and two of his brothers that weekend. We hit a few local bars, and we went to their clubhouse for a beer. Lucky and I would keep in touch throughout the years. He has since left his club for his own personal reasons.

March 7, 2008. I headed down to Daytona again. Why not? It was winter in New Jersey. I stopped in to see CC and the Long County brothers on the way. That's what's awesome about our club. A clubhouse and brothers are always close by for us to stop and have a place to stay even if they weren't the destination. On the way home, I decided to take the long way and banged a left on Route 10 then went north to visit our Opelika chapter then onto North Georgia before heading home.

For those that don't know, I work for Passaic Valley Sewerage Commission. I'm a state employee. I have been there since June 1999. I love my job, and the benefits are the best. One of them being the time off. Now twenty-two years later, I get five weeks' vacation a year. Back then, I got only three. But when I work overtime, I can take it as time off. So if I work eight hours of overtime, I can get twelve hours of "time due" instead of time and a half pay. I have started years with over eleven weeks of time off between my vacation, personal, and time due hours. It has been a blessing, allowing me to travel as much as I want. I thank God for my job multiple times a day.

April 16, 2008. Coyote (prospect from Orange County), George, and I headed to Long County for the pimp and hoe ball. The party was a great time. The locals where all amped up for the weekend, and a lot of brothers showed up from out of town. I had met this broad we will call her Denise a few months back and had her meet me in Long County for the weekend. Now, Friday night I was in my bed in the hotel right around the corner from the clubhouse. Brother Pork Chop from Beaufort, South Carolina, chapter and his wife were in the room next to me. Well, brother Pork Chop can snore, I mean fucking snore. I sleep with earplugs, and it was still brutal to hear in my room. I got out of bed and banged on his door and told him to roll over or something. He just said, "Sorry, Butta." Well, fast-forward to Saturday night and Denise and I in the room. Let's just say, she is a little exaggerated with her vocals during sex. All of a sudden, Pork Chop was banging on my door, yelling, "I can't fucking snore, but I got to hear 'Fuck me, Butta' all night?" I apologized and told her to keep it down. God bless you, brother Pork Chop. You are sorely missed.

I remember two very specific things on the ride home that Sunday. First, when George, Coyote, and I left at around 0400 hours Sunday morning, we were on 84, heading to the 95. We saw up ahead a car coming west toward us, and he was swerving. I shouted to George (and Coyote) to wait till he got closer, then we got all the way over to the right. He went by right on the yellow lines, and we saw the driver was out cold, head back, mouth open, dead asleep or just dead! Always expect the unexpected!

It started raining at around the bottom end of Maryland. I mean raining. We were dead stopped in traffic on the 95, and the water rolling down the highway was actually coming over our boots! Then, all of a sudden, there was a huge thunder crash and a huge bolt of lightning. George looked over at me and said, "I knew we were missing something!" You had to be there; it was funny at the time. We made it home wet, but without incident.

May 15, 2008. A bunch of us from Bergen went up to a bar/restaurant in Rockland to meet up with Rockland brothers. Chachie was dating some psycho he met through a brother from down south's daughter, and it was her birthday. Maybe it was his. I really can't remember. But what I do remember was, she wanted to marry him. She tattooed Vinny (Chachie's real name) and her name across her back on, like, their second date. Yeah, she was a keeper, all right. Anyway, I thought it would be funny if I bought them a "congratulations on your engagement" card! You know, just as a good prank. We got there, and they were all already sitting at the table. I handed Chachie the card. Well, when it was opened, she gasped, and Chachie looked at me like I just had sex with his mother (which I actually did a few times). I then proceeded to bury the hatchet by saying, "Oh my god, you didn't ask her yet?" She started screaming, "Yes, yes, of course, I'll marry you," and Chachie was a statue, just staring into the abyss. Yeah, I ruined the dinner when he had to tell her it was a prank and he wasn't proposing!

May 22, 2008. A bunch of us from Bergen headed to Phenix City for nationals. Had a great time with brothers. They gave us really nice-looking bottles of homemade wine a brother made. On the way home, little Kenny decided we were drinking the bottles of wine that we were taking back for the brothers who could not make the trip. That was the worst-tasting wine I have ever had. I still have my full bottle.

On the ride back, Kenny's bike was losing charging capabilities. So every gas stop we had to push him to start his bike. Last gas stop was at the border of Pennsylvania and New Jersey; it was mine and Darren's turn to push. It was, like, ninety degrees and humid. Well, Darren and I pushed. Kenny hit the clutch. Nothing. We pushed him the other way. Kenny hit the clutch. Nothing. We started pushing him back the other way again when I noticed Kenny nonchalantly reach down and turn on his ignition. Just as Darren went to smack him in the head, he dropped the clutch. The bike roared to life, and he took off, cracking up while Darren missed with his swing. *Good bikes, good friends, good times, and bad women!*

July 3, 2008. Myself, Ed from Orange County, and PD from Long County headed to Fayetteville for the annual Fourth of July party. PD came from Georgia to Bergen to ride down with me. Really, he was padding his run miles, taking aim at winning Captain Wingmen that year. I remember stopping for gas in Virginia, and PD bought us all a Harley-Davidson scratch-off lottery ticket. Well, great intentions; however, we were at that gas station for, like, an hour. I would win $20 and go buy more tickets for all of us. Then Ed would win, and again, we were scratching tickets. This went on for a while till, yeah, we won nothing.

Fayetteville was a blast. Hot as fuck, but always a good time. Walter, a brother from Fayetteville, is the grill master extraordinaire. He can cook on a grill for sure. I ended up hooking up with a woman. We'll call her Mary (she will come up again later). She was friends with Rosie and Sue from the Moore County national weekend the year before. She told me they both had given me good grades, so she wanted to see for herself. It's always good to try to leave an impression, brothers. It just may pay off down the road.

Sunday morning was calling for thunderstorms all day up and down the East Coast. I told Ed, if we didn't want to get slammed, we had to leave at, like, 0300 hours Sunday morning. Well, Ed decided he would take his chances and roll out around 1000 hours. Well, I made it home in the pouring rain by 1130 hours. Ed got home two days later. He left at 1000 hours and got a way up the 95 and then came to a roadblock. They had the highway shut down due to flooding. He then decided to take side roads and two-lane highways north. Now, remember, this was before GPS went and spoiled our asses. We used to tape maps to our gas tanks if we didn't know the route by heart. No robot voice telling you when to turn, no "recalculating." Either way made for a great laugh and some lines in this book.

August 1, 2008. Myself, Ed from Orange, and my friend Joanne (Big Red) all rode down to Fayetteville together for Lee Carrillo's twenty-fifth anniversary party. Joanne had just bought a Sportster and asked me a month or so before if I were taking a trip could she ride along. We decided Fayetteville would be the best since they are only 550 miles away. We all met at my house and hit the Turnpike south. I have to say, I was very impressed. She rode like a pro and didn't have any issues at all riding down. I have a great picture of us at a gas stop. Her face was covered in road grime, and she had the biggest smile on her face.

Kelli had come up to meet me in Fayetteville. That Friday night I decided to introduce Joanne to my brother Juan "Ditch" Lopez. I wanted to get to spend time with Kelli and go do dinner and a ride. Plus, I knew I'd be busy, and I didn't want to leave Joanne to fend for herself among my heathen brothers. Joanne was a Bergen girl. She had never traveled to another chapter. She met a few brothers when they would come to Bergen for an event. But for the most part, she didn't know anyone. I told Ditch, "She isn't a whore and isn't looking to get laid. She is a very good friend of mine, so treat her with respect." Well, a few years later, they would marry and have babies and buy houses and RVs, and yeah, I can claim fame to that. Ditch and Joanne, I love you both very much.

August 13, 2008. This day started an epic journey which had me on the road on my bike for eleven days. The only reason it ended on the eleventh day was, I had to go to the hospital. Here is my best recollection of the events. I headed to Fayetteville to hang out with brothers. I stayed at Chachie's house. I wanted to puncture my eardrums. "Enough about me. Let's talk about me" was Chachie's mantra. I did get a great history lesson on Rockland, but the trade-off was only stories involving Chachie. From Chachie's house, I headed to Long County. I had to meet with our national sergeant at arms, Von Zipper, and take care of a few things. Spent some time with CC and his family. Later that night Zipper and I tag teamed one of his local stable girls. My god, this girl was cute as ever but as dumb as your left foot. I mean downright just stupid. However, we bonded as brothers and had a great time.

The next morning, Zipper, Albie, and I headed to Oak Grove. Now, if you have never ridden with Albie before, learn from these next few lines. I love Albie. He is one of my closest and dearest brothers. But, man, does he take his time when going somewhere. I mean, we would ride, like, thirty miles and get off the highway. I'd pull up to him and ask, "What's up?" He would always respond, "There's this joint up the road. They make the best Bloody Marys!" He also knew every single barmaid in all the places we would stop. Then when we were actually on the road, left lane, sixty miles an hour! Maybe it's because he nor Zipper had jobs at the time? I don't know, but man, they were killing me.

We arrive in Oak Grove and settled into our hotel rooms. My civilian friend, James, met me there. He and I were rooming together. Friday night was at the clubhouse, and Saturday was at the barn. This was my first pistol shoot as a competitor. Now, living in the Northeast Communist Bloc of the United States of America, I wasn't able to travel "legally" with a gun. This was one of the few times I didn't. I had CC bring me a pistol to shoot. Now CC had this competition Kimber .45 ACP that's worth, like, well over a grand that he is using. He handed me this old rusted 1911. I looked at the gun then looked at him, and he said, "You didn't think I would give you something you could beat me with, did you?" Way to go, C. Joanne "Big Red" had ridden down by herself. She was supposed to ride with a couple brothers from Bergen, but their plans didn't pan out. Credit where credit is due. She had only owned a bike for a few months, and she rode around eight hundred miles to see my brother Ditch.

Now Joanne and I are and were always just friends. But I still felt I was owed something for the obvious relationship that was beginning from Phenix City or Ditch for my part in all this. I could've introduced her to Roy the Ambo of fun, and she would've been ruined for life. So I decided I wanted brother Jake from Phenix Cities Fedora. It was a beauty. So I got a new hat, Ditch got to marry his soul mate a few years later, and Jake was out a hat! Seems fair to me. If it's any consolation, I still have the hat!

Now keep in mind, I'm a Marine. I don't shoot handguns. I shoot rifles. I might as well throw the handgun at you then shoot it at you. But I am a very competitive person. I missed third place in two events by only one point. I was pretty impressed with my performance. CC took first in one event and second in another, I believe.

Now, the plan was, sometime on Sunday James and I were heading back to his house in Kernersville. I was going to do an oil change on the bike, and we would chill and do some fishing on his boat. Then I would be heading to Hotlanta to hook up with brother Roy Willy to continue this adventure.

Now, like I said, I was picking and choosing when to drink for maximum effectiveness and when not to. I wanted to be a leader in this nation, and to do so, I believe you have to lead by example. If you're always a drunken mess, no one will ever take you seriously.

Well, this Saturday night was a good one to do so. Not too many civilians were there, and no other clubs in attendance. Best yet was, I didn't have to get up at the ass crack of dawn and ride eight hundred or so miles home for once. So I proceed to drink tequila with CC all night. Got a ride in a cage to the room where James had been out cold for hours already. Well, I got out of bed Sunday morning, and James was giving me the "I told you so" about drinking.

I then looked at him and told him, "My bike is at the barn. You have to take me there."

He looked at me, knowing what was about to take place next, and said, "How all we have is my bike?"

I smiled and said, "Yes, we do." I folded my kutte and put it in his saddle bag and hopped on the back. Yeah, I got a killer selfie of that little three-mile ride.

We got to James's house late that afternoon and worked on the bikes a bit. We went to this excellent BBQ place that I can't remember the name of. Then next morning, we woke up early and headed to the lake and took his boat out for a while and did some bass fishing. I love spending time with James; we don't get to do it often enough.

So I headed out in the morning and rolled to Phenix City and met up with Roy. We rode to Atlanta's Hartsfield-Jackson Atlanta International Airport. We had good intel that our brother Stew from Devil's Elbow, who was now to be residing in Gainesville with our North Georgia chapter, was flying in from Germany on some leave.

I will never forget the look on his soon to be ex-wife's face when we walked and stood next to her at the gate. She knew right then and there she wouldn't be spending any time with her husband anytime soon! Stew saw us and gave us hugs then looked at his wife and asked if she had fed us. She just walked away. We all met at Stew's house. He grabbed his kutte, and we all rode to a tattoo parlor at the southside of Atlanta. That is where I met the infamous "Uncle Billy." Uncle Billy is CC's blood uncle (his mother's brother). Stew and Roy had met him and knew him well. Uncle Billy is a piercer by trade and at the time was a partner in the tattoo shop. Uncle Billy was a civilian; however, he would go on to become a Wingmen in the future. We all walked down the street a bit and had lunch together.

After lunch, myself and Roy hit it hard to Dawson County from Atlanta. That is usually an hour and fifteen-minute ride. We made it in forty-five minutes. We hung out in Dawson's clubhouse for the night with Robo, Bones, Bob, Smokey, DJ, and a few others. This was the original clubhouse, and I remember Robo being so proud of the contraption that made flat beer not flat anymore. That was the first time in my life I drank real homemade moonshine from a jar. It would become one of my favorite drinks.

Next morning Roy and I looked at the weather and decided, "Let's go to Opelika." On the way there, Roy told me he was taking me to this awesome place to have lunch. We rolled off a two-lane and onto a tar and chipped road, which then turned to a dirt road. I was thinking we were lost, and all of a sudden, there was this little shack with a sign that read "Paul's Place." We went in, and I looked at the one-page, one-sided menu and saw they had what they called the "Paul's Favorite!" It is a fried spam and cheese on a hamburger roll! I had to try it, and I remember taking a picture of the menu for keepsake to show the New Jersey people the places I've opened myself to by becoming a Wingmen!

We sat in on Opelika's church that night. There was an old guy sitting at the bar we were talking to for a while; his name was Roy also. His nickname was Birdie. Nice enough guy, I thought. Well, in church Gary from Opelika called for a vote to stand up their hang-around, Birdie. Now Roy and I looked at each other and thought, *The really old guy?* I try to make it a point not to talk in another chapter's church, but I raised my hand and was called upon to speak.

I asked, "The really old guy at the bar Birdie?"

Gary said, "Yes, why?"

I just shrugged and said, "Never mind."

I'm against talking in another chapter's church, and I'm very against prospecting old guys. So I was in a dilemma. I believe you have a right to grow old in the club, but I don't think bringing in an old guy who most likely can't defend our patch or himself is a good idea. I have been very vocal about this throughout the years. I decided not to push it and just shut up. I figured I would give them the "I told you so" later on down the road. However, that opportunity never came. I must say, Birdie who did prospect and patch out has been the exception to the rule. He is a solid brother and very dear to me. He has helped me through some rough shit and has always answered the call when called upon. Other than shooting Charles in the face, he has a perfect Wingmen record!

That night we partied in the clubhouse, and back then Opelika had a barmaid named Marcia (not her real name). Not bad-looking, late thirty something (I think). Well, I was in the head, taking a piss, when Roy popped his head in, and then he let Marcia come in behind him. Roy said, "She would like to blow you. I got the door."

All I could think about was how dirty the floor was that she was kneeling on.

From Opelika, we headed up to Calhoun County for their first anniversary party. Aimee was there because that is the chapter Ron was in. Uncle Billy showed up with a tattoo artist, and they were servicing people who wanted ink and piercings. The old clubhouse on Tenth Street was massive. It was an old warehouse. Lee and Albie were there. Hell, I think half the nation was there.

I was hanging with Ditch, Country, Wil, Ivan, Dirty Dick Dino, Fat Mike, Chopper, and Jake when a civilian was making some claims about the Seventy-Fifth Ranger Battalion. Well, that caught Ditch and Jake's attention, and they went over and started grilling the guy. Well, apparently, the guy didn't have the cheat sheet right for Ditch and Jake's test. It was obvious he served, just not to the capacity of what he was claiming. They were getting ready to hammer this guy for obviously lying about his military career. I walked over and asked them two to excuse themselves and I would handle the situation. Now, it's not that I didn't want the guy to get his face caved in for lying; it's because it was Calhoun's first big party, and usually a civilian getting stomped—which is what the Phenix City "Fight Club" was fixing to do—usually puts an early end to a party.

I introduced myself to this guy, and he was around six feet, two hundred or so pounds.

I said to him, "I served in the Marine reserves and the National Guard, and there is no shame in what you did or didn't do in the military. Just don't lie to guys who do it for a living it kinda pisses them off."

I told him to finish his beer like a man and I would walk him out to his bike, car, or call him a cab (no Uber back then) if need be. Now, I was standing to his right with my right side to the bar. He was facing the bar with both hands on the bar.

He faced me and said, "What if I don't want to leave?"

I chuckled and said, "Are you really going to go there? Don't mistake my kindness for weakness."

He then threw his arms out to the sides and over his shoulders and said, "Well, fuck you, and fuck your club."

I had my right elbow on the bar, all ready to throw the straight good-night right hand. I hit him before he even knew what was going on. He was out before he hit the floor.

Dirty Dick Dino and Fat Mike were getting ready to put boots to him, and Ivan yelled, "Enough. Butta ended it. Leave him be."

They dragged him outside. I grabbed my beer and faced the bar and saw my friend Aimee looking at me and smiling (she loves fights). I tipped my beer to her, and that was when I noticed his front tooth sticking out of my middle finger knuckle!

I believe it was Brother Elwood who took me in the back room and cleaned the wound and dressed it for me. I was happy the crowd didn't disperse over the incident, but it had to be done for the disrespect he showed myself and our club. I think I handled the situation as best as could be with as little collateral damage as possible.

I returned to my room, and my hand was throbbing. Now, remember, I had to ride almost a thousand miles the next day. I woke up at zero dark thirty, and rain was coming down sideways. I packed the bike and threw on my rain gear. I stopped and fueled up then jumped on Route 20. The weather channel said, once I got to Atlanta, it would stop. Now, I was riding and riding, and it was getting worse and worse. Wind was picking up, and I was like, *What the fuck, weatherman?* Remember, pre-GPS days! I then realized I was going west when, of course, I needed to be going east! I flipped a U-turn, and before you know it, I needed fuel again. Yes, that's how far I went in the wrong direction in a storm in the middle of the night! I got off an exit, and lo and behold, it was the same gas station I fueled up at a few hours before! I went inside, and the attendant had this puzzled look on his face. He went to say something, and I just said, "Don't you say a fucking word."

By Atlanta the rain stopped, and the rest of the ride home was awesome, except the swelling and the pain in my hand. The last gas stop in Pennsylvania, it hurt so bad I had to ask someone to fuel my bike for me. I got home, jumped in the shower, and told Lucille she had to take me to the hospital. I get admitted in the ER, and they did an x-ray. Next thing I know, this nurse was rushing me back to the bed and sticking me with an IV. The doctor came in to inform me my hand was not broken.

I say, "Great news. What's with the IV?"

"The bad news is, you have a staph infection."

Well, I ended up in the hospital for six fucking days! At one point, they were talking about amputating my hand if the infection didn't start breaking up!

The morning of the sixth day, I told the doctor I had to leave. He said the infection had finally started to break, and he didn't advise that. I explained I was in a motorcycle club and that I travel all over the country. I then explained Rockland County, New York, chapter was hosting our national Labor Day meeting, and there was no way I was missing a national meeting, especially one right in my backyard! I finally got him to agree to let me go home with a pic line to my heart hanging out of my armpit. I had to give myself ampicillin three times a day for another eighteen days afterward till the infection finally went away. The most expensive punch I ever threw. Never aim for the mouth. Never. It's also why I prefer elbows over punches.

August 29, 2008. Rockland was hosting the September national. This was still in the old firehouse clubhouse. Bergen had a prospect by the name of "Tiny." He was six feet, six inches tall. His main job was to follow me around, holding my IV bag when it was time to juice myself up.

September 29, 2008. It is inevitable in this lifestyle to never experience the next trip and story. I got a phone call at around 1800 hours from brother Weird Al from Oak Grove chapter that our brother Wil was in a bad wreck and being life flighted to Vanderbilt hospital in Nashville, Tennessee. My heart sank. Wil was one of my closest brothers. I grabbed a few things and jumped on my bike in the pouring rain. I rode hard and fast and got to the hospital mid-morning. The Oak Grove brothers were there along with Wil's wife and his baby's momma. Yeah, Wil was the ladies' man for sure. The news on his condition was not good. He had serious brain trauma, and they had to cut out part of his skull to release the pressure on his brain. The next day, they allowed me into the ICU to see him. If it weren't for his tattoos, I would've never known it was him. I stayed another couple of days till he was out of ICU.

October 8, 2008. I headed back to Nashville to visit Wil. He was doing much better and was giving the staff a real hard time. It was obvious the head shot had made Wil a little more far off than he normally was. He had a few days where he would try to escape from the hospital, thinking he was a POW. I was wheeling him around in a wheelchair, and he, all of a sudden, grabbed my hand and told me to pick him up and make a run for the stairwell. He was serious and got pissed when I brought him back to his room. He told me it was on me if we didn't survive the night.

Wil was an incredible man. He was a decorated combat veteran with a borderline genius IQ. One minute he is washing his bike, listening to Metallica; the next he is drinking expensive whiskey, reading Plato, while listening to Mozart. What I loved most about Wil was, he didn't judge anyone. I speak of him here in past tense 'cause though he survived and recovered from this wreck, he would later have another from which he wouldn't survive.

A few days later, Albie and Zipper came to the hospital to see Wil. He told them I was a dick for not breaking us out when we had the chance. We hung with Wil for the day with his parents, then the three of us headed to Devil's Elbow.

We got there eventually, you know, feeding Albie his Bloody Marys along the way! Funny thing happened. We were to meet a few brothers at a casino right over the river in Illinois. We were just a block away from the casino's parking lot, and I said we should fuel up now as to not have to in the morning. We pulled in, and while I was taking my gas cap off, this little convertible pulled to the other side of the pump I was using. Well, this woman got out with these little shorts on and a pair of legs that belonged with the Rockettes. I went into Joey mode and give her the "how you doin'?" We started chatting, and now I was really not paying attention as to what I was doing. She too was heading to the casino. I handed her my Wingmen business card and hoped for the best.

So I jumped on my bike, started it up, dropped it in first gear, and took off like a bat out of hell. I got about five hundred feet, and all of a sudden, white smoke was pouring out of my exhaust. I had no power to the engine, and I thought, *Oh shit, I just dropped an exhaust valve and or blew a head gasket.* We coasted into the casino parking lot. I stopped the bike. Zipper asked me to start it up again, and he made pretty much the same assessment I did; we both thought it was an exhaust valve or gasket. Now I was pissed off. I was supposed to go into a poker tournament that cost $300 to buy in. I didn't have a warranty anymore on the bike, and I thought, *My weekend is ruined, and how am I going to get home?*

Well, the beauty about being part of a nation is, you have brothers everywhere and they're always willing to help. We called a retired brother who lived right in Saint Louis. His name is Ben. He called the local dealership. They made plans to leave someone behind. He came by with his truck and trailer. We loaded up the Softail, and off he went to the dealership.

Now I decided I couldn't get into this tournament because I didn't know how much it was going to cost to fix the bike, so I made a bad decision of getting hammered drunk. We were in the casino bar, and one of the bartenders was of Asian descent. I introduced myself to him and shook his hand, and without letting go, I asked him if he knew karate. He replied no, and I said, "Good because I'm probably going to be belligerent tonight." Next thing I know, Albie was tapping me on the shoulder to turn around. I noticed casino security sent over four guys, and they were pulling a semicircle around us, watching us very intently. I decided after four or five double jacks to confront them and let them know there weren't enough of them and they were not getting paid enough money! Next thing you know, there were about twelve security guards pulling a semicircle of security around us! I fronted one of them and told him I beat guys up like him on the way to a fight. Albie came over, put his arm around me, and said, "Brother, if you want to do this, you know we're all down, but we have really, really nice rooms, and I would really like to stay here tonight." I asked him in slurred voice if he would feed me and if he would get me cheesecake, he agreed, and that's all it took to turn that night into a good night instead of a night in jail, waiting for bail.

The next morning, a brother named Cowboy from our Miller County, Missouri, chapter showed up to take me to Devil's Elbow chapter. We had not gotten out of the parking lot when I got a phone call from the dealership.

The guy on the other end of the phone said, "I have good news, and I have bad news."

I said, "Give me the bad news first."

He said, "Your bike will not run on diesel."

I said, "What is the good news?"

He said, "The good news is, you owe me $40. The bike is ready to go."

So Cowboy headed for the dealership, and about two hours later, I was pulling into Devil's Elbow, being greeted by a big, giant cardboard sign that said, "Diesel bikes park here. This means you, Butta." I love my brothers! Apparently, I loaded her with diesel while trying to get legs to meet me in the casino. By the way, she never showed. Double the pain.

October ?, 2008. I never wrote this event down because it is not something to be repeated and really was a crazy night that could've ended in absolute tragedy to include death and definite jail time. With that being said, it was one of the best nights I've ever had as a *Wingmen*!

I was at Bergen's clubhouse with George, drinking whiskey and taking Valium. I was in a particularly bad mood, thinking about our brother Wil and his condition. I decided to call Lucille and told her to pick up George and I and take us to Orange County. We had been drinking, and going to hang out in Orange with Chaz and Murry was what I needed at that moment. We went up there, and there were only a few people there: Chaz, Murry, Odd Todd, Prospect Coyote, some broad Chaz was banging, and her girlfriend. Well, at some point, and for some reason only known by Nighttime Chaz, he instructed the prospect to give him the shotgun from under the bar. The prospect handed it to him, and Chaz yelled, "I'm fucking telling you that fucking boar's head has a camera in its eye!" Then he racked the gun and blew the boar's head off the wall from above the front door. Everyone hit the floor except for Chaz, Murry, and myself. I looked, and George was on the floor, facedown. I grabbed the gun from Chaz, racked it, and proceeded to put it to the back of Gorge's head and say, "Get the fuck up. You're making Bergen look like pussies." (Yeah, I was that fucked up!) After that it was on from just blowing holes in the floor, walls, and furniture to playing shotgun soccer with the boar's head in the front parking lot.

Now, I don't condone this behavior. It was fucked up (we were fucked up), and I really don't know how (1) no one got shot or killed and (2) the cops were never called. There were homes right next to and across from that clubhouse.

The next morning, Lucille, George, and myself were in an IHOP back in New Jersey, eating. George and I were almost sober now. I asked Lucille where she was parked again while we were there. When we went back out to her Durango. There were two slug holes in the rear quarter panel right by the gas tank filler!

The three of us took a lot of shit for our actions, and all three of us were fined $375 each. Forty-five casings—that was how many empties were counted, and we were subsequently fined $25 for each one divided by three.

Real stupid, but what a memory and what a crazy night it was for sure. I don't think I have ever seen Fireman John since that event without him smacking me in the head for it.

October 25, 2008. Brother PD from Long County came up to Bergen and stayed at my house for a few days. That weekend we, along with Kenny, Darren, and Albie, rode up to Orange County for a chapter barbecue. PD was trying his hardest to rack up miles to compete with me for this year's Captain Wingmen award. It was harder for PD to get the miles because his distances were a lot shorter to get to. My average ride to a clubhouse back then was around eight hundred miles each way. His was probably around 250 to 350.

We had a blast up in Orange as usual. Chaz went nighttime on us, and all was right in the world. I miss that chapter. Many great times and memories up there.

October 30, 2008. I headed to Fayetteville for Halloween. This was the first trip I ever took Lucille on to date. Most brothers didn't really think I was married and that I was just making it up. Well, we were at Lee's wife Diane's sister's bar, and all was good when, all of a sudden, Rosie from Rick James's house incident ran up to me and jumped on me and wrapped her legs around me and said, "I'm so glad you're here. I really need to get laid!" Well, I put her feet back on the floor and then introduced her to my wife. She turned red and apologized and said she was only kidding. Lucille took it in stride and just replied, looking at me, "Well, at least she's cute." She was a trooper, all right.

December 5, 2008. We patched out Tiny that night. Tiny and George were both guys I worked with. I did not encourage them to stand up, only to come down and support our parties. Tiny was a Fierce Allegiance patch holder with me for a short while before deciding to step down along with me. They both, however, started asking what it takes to become a Wingmen, and both ended up standing up eventually. I must say, both were model prospects. However, both turned into idiots once patched. George was nothing short of moronic when alcohol was added to his bloodstream. Couldn't keep his mouth shut no matter what.

One day George ran his mouth to some civilians even after being told to just let the matter be. Said some things that they were able to manipulate and put us in a situation with another club. Trust me, he was wrong, and it is hard to defend wrong. I was president of the chapter at the time. I handled the situation without incident with the other club. Then I handled George. I ended up knocking one of his molars out on the left side of his mouth with my right elbow. I explained to him that previous fines and a suspension he hadn't learned from, so maybe a little tough love would help. Well, it did, all right. He quit a week or so later.

Now I think that is a positive outcome. Some brothers will argue with me on my ways of certain discipline. But when it finally comes to having to put your hands on a brother for "learning" purposes, you do so without taking it too far. Then after the fact, it is over. No gloating. You don't bring it up again. Don't run and tell other brothers what transpired. It's over. You hug, have a beer, and start over fresh. If he learns from it, great. If he quits, great. Either way, the club will not have to deal with a patch holder who is not living the Wingmen way. Bergen County has learned to use this method over the years, and we have always gotten the desired results. Some fix themselves. Some go pussy and quit. Either way, we got what we wanted, a better Wingmen, or we got rid of someone we thought would be a good Wingmen.

Tiny was pretty much the same story. Only his stupidness involved thinking every woman in the room wanted him when you added alcohol to his bloodstream.

I had this barmaid in my stable named Farrah. She was a great girl. Worked at the strip club around the corner from our clubhouse that was on Romanelli in South Hackensack. She never called. She always waited for me to initiate contact. Whenever we rolled into the bar, she hooked us up with drinks all night long, etc. Well, one Sunday I was caging it back from Calhoun County (I had left one of my bikes there for the upcoming winter; I spent a lot of time there) with Little Billy (a hang-around at the time). I get a text from Farrah, "911." Apparently, Tiny was there, and he was telling her I told him it was all right for him and her to hook up. Anyway, long story short, if he would've actually asked me, I would've made the call for him, and he would've gotten what he wanted. However, lying and using my name like that really pissed me off. (Also, this was not the first time Tiny and women-associated problems plagued Bergen County. He had already been fined, suspended, and a few brothers had already smacked him a few times.) I told her she was free, White, and over twenty-one, and if she wanted to, no problem. She wasn't interested, and now I wouldn't ask her to be since he went behind my back and lied.

I asked her to hand Tiny the phone. I told him to leave the bar, and I would stop by his home on my way home. Billy and I got there at, like, 2200 hours. He came outside, and I ripped into him, and he only made it worse by lying and tried to tell me he wasn't even there. Apparently, he was so drunk earlier he forgot he spoke to me on her phone from the bar. So he caught an elbow. A few months later, he pissed off Johhny Crash, and Johhny lit him up. Then a while later, prospect Jay and him went at it. Tiny was one of those patch holders that constantly shit on prospects. Don't know why because he wasn't treated that way, but hey, for whatever reason, he looked at prospects like they were a bad odor. So one night Jay had had enough and called him out. He put the boots to Tiny pretty good, and then Tiny quit. Problem solved.

Moral of the stories: your true self will come out sooner or later. Brain once told me, "Butta, it may take five days, five months, or twenty-five years. If they are not being themselves while prospecting, sooner or later it will surface, and they will be gone." Truth.

That pretty much rounds out the year of 2008. I once again hit my goal set to ride over twenty thousand miles. I ended the year with 20,907 miles with my eagle on my back. I visited out-of-state chapters that year seventeen times.

C H A P T E R   9

Year "Three"

My goal once again was to ride twenty thousand plus miles for 2009. Also, I changed my spending ways and wanted a new bagger by years end.

January 15, 2009. Myself, Barry, and Tiny headed down to Fayetteville for January national. There were snowstorms by us and ice storms in North Carolina, so we caged. PD won Captain Wingmen, and I was very proud of him. He was way behind me in miles, but he hit almost double the run scheduled events as I had. That's a lot of weekends away from home and dedication to supporting the nation.

January 19, 2009. The following weekend, I rode down to hang out with my good friend, James. We had Dani and Kim from Virginia meet us at his house, and we had a great time. We hit a few gun shows and went shopping and shooting. I remember piling into his golf cart at, like, three in the morning, all liquored up, making the neighbors wish his White trash ass didn't move in! James bought this monsterlike, 3,500-square-foot home in a gated community where a bunch of NASCAR drivers lived. Man, did they hate him when I visited.

Anyway, it was great to spend time with James, Dani, and Kim. I always wished James and I lived closer to each other, but doesn't seem like it will ever be the case. He is retired now and living in western North Carolina again after moving all over the country for the past twenty or so years for his work.

January 24, 2009. A night I won't ever forget. Bergen was having an open house, and the place was packed. We have great civilian support up here. I got a call toward the end of the night from brother Animal from our Beaufort chapter to inform me our brother Pork Chop was in a wreck and didn't survive his injuries. It was like a punch to the face. Instantly sobering, I remember calling Bergen brothers one by one into the meeting room to inform them of the situation.

I always say, live life to the fullest, brothers. Let the ones know who you love that you love them. Let the ones know who you think are dicks that you think they are dicks. You never know when you're not going to wake up for the next day.

January 30, 2009. Myself, Creepy Dave, and Todd caged down to Beaufort South Carolina for our brother's funeral. Man, if you didn't get to know Pork, you missed out. He was a great brother and had a wicked sense of humor. He was always smiling, always upbeat and positive.

I remember, a few weeks later, calling my tattoo artist, and I told him I wanted a tat of a pork chop. He asked if I wanted it like cartoonish. I said, no, just a pork chop. He never disappointed. He drew a stencil from a ShopRite coupon of a pork chop. The ink is on my left wrist. Love you, Pork. Miss you dearly, brother WFFW.

February 19, 2009. I ended up selling my Softail classic to Angela. She used to date our brother Roundy from Savannah. With that money and the country's economy in the shitter due to the scumbag, traitor president the weak people of the country voted in. I took advantage of a great job, credit score, and poor economy and bought the infamous "Ms. Bettie." She is a 2009 black Ultra Classic. All the bells and whistles, and she was going to put in some work for sure over the next years.

April 2, 2009. I headed down to Phenix City for their fifth anniversary party. The winter was a wet one in New Jersey, and I hadn't really been able to put any miles on Bettie. So I scheduled my thousand-mile service at Columbus Harley-Davidson for that Saturday morning.

That morning, riding to Columbus, I realized how great anti-lock brakes are. I was a little hung over and tired still and not paying too much attention. Then I realized I had to get over 'cause my exit was a left exit. I came in hot! Realized I had to jam the breaks and hope for the best at the last second. They did their job and definitely saved me from at best just a bad wreck.

I left ass crack of dawn on Sunday. While I was riding through town to get to the interstate, some dude was burning leaves in his yard. I mean he had a frigging bonfire going. There was this big-ass column of smoke stretching right across the roadway I ended up riding through. Well, a few hundred or so miles later, I started itching bad, everywhere on my frigging body. By the time I got home, I was covered from head to toe in poison ivy! I must have breathed it in and had a bad allergic reaction to it. I mean it was everywhere. In between my toes, in my nose, ears, *everywhere*!

April 15, 2009. I headed down to North Georgia for Uncle Billy's patching. I had to cage it because I was still fucked up with the poison ivy. I met brother Gabe who is now in our Phenix City chapter. We hit it off, and he talked me into going too Long County for the pimp and hoe ball. Brother KJ from Long County let me ride his bike from North Georgia to Long County. Railroad and KJ drove my Kia Rio.

April 14, 2009. I headed out to Devil's Elbow to attend brother OB's wedding. Of course, it rained almost the whole way there. We all partied and hung out at the clubhouse Friday night. Saturday morning, we were all to meet at the club house for 0800 hours kickstands up to ride to OB's farm for the wedding.

CC and I decided to go get breakfast at the little diner right next to our hotel. When I tell you hillbilly central, my god. The waitress was like ninety years old and knew every person there. It took her like twenty minutes just to get to our table to take our order. CC kept telling me to relax. See, in the north, you go to a restaurant, they take your order, bring you food, you eat, pay, and leave. In the South, there is no frigging rush for them to do any of the above! When she finally came back around from talking to everyone again, she took our order. I politely explained to her we had to be somewhere in like twenty minutes. Anyone that knows me well knows if I say 1700 hours, I really mean 1630 hours. To me, if you're on time, you're late. It literally makes my eye twitch to be late! CC keeps reassuring me to relax, we wouldn't be late. Well, we were late getting back to the clubhouse, and the steak with my eggs was freezer burned. I still think that bitch gave me that one on purpose.

Well, lo and behold, we got to the clubhouse, and not even half the brothers were there, nevertheless ready to ride. CC looked at me and said, "I told you not to worry. Wingmen time is alive and well today!" We had a nice pack of around fifty or so bikes. Great weather and great time was had by all.

On the way home CC, Trucker Tom, and I decided to stop off at Harrah's Casino to do a little gambling. Our trip was cut short when we got a call that night that our brothers PD and Country's dad had passed. We rode to Long County in the morning to support our brothers.

I stayed in Long County for the week to attend the funeral, and Long County was hosting nationals the following weekend. Didn't make sense to go home to come back. Got to get some good time in with brothers while not a lot was going on.

June 5, 2009. Darren and I headed to Moore County for their annual rodeo. It was the first time being held on the clubhouse property and not at the old fairgrounds. It was still a great party with all the usual rodeo events. It was determined though that Moore County needed to upgrade their air-conditioning unit that weekend!

June 26, 2009. Myself, Barry, Tiny, Frankie the Elbow, and RB headed up to Orange County for "Talking John's" going-away party. He was transferring to our new Pax, West Virginia, chapter. We really went to be sure John was really going and didn't change his mind! He is called Talking John for a reason! If you ever have an hour or so of your life you really don't need, say hello to talking John!

July 2, 2009. Darren, Kenny, and myself headed down to Fayetteville for their annual Fourth of July party. It's hot as balls as usual. Had a great time and got to spend some time with brother's home from deployments. About twenty or so of us hit one of the buffet places in town for lunch on Saturday. Walter was pissed because he had been cooking barbecue all day. I think we really went just to escape the heat.

This was the weekend I approached Lee and Albie, who were at the time our national president and national vice president. I expressed my wanting to do more for the nation and asked if they would consider me for the position of regional sergeant at arms. Now I was the president of Bergen and would have to vacate that position which I loved. But I felt I could contribute more to the nation at the next level. After some talking and answering of some good questions, Lee decided he would give me a shot at doing the job. This was the beginning of a very long working relationship between Lee and myself.

I was excited and ready to take on the challenge of the new position. The club was growing at this time, and I knew there would be a lot of riding and work to be done. First thing I did was limit my partying to only when around our own even more. I had to lead by example even more now. I would be involved with other chapters business, not just Bergen's now. I was up for the challenge.

July 17, 2009. Igor, Ronnie, Todd, Kenny, prospect Al, and myself all rode up to Rockland. They were patching out the "Vulture" Timmy. Timmy is a great brother and Wingmen. I was very happy for him and wouldn't have missed it. With that said, now SHUT THE FUCK UP, TIMMY!

July 30, 2009. We had a couple guys hanging around for a while. They were attending our open houses and other events then started coming around on Friday nights as well. They were Jay and Little Billy. The previous week, we had an open house, and I told them they were coming with me on a four-day trip to visit some chapters. They gladly agreed.

We hit Fayetteville first then headed down to Savannah. That was the weekend we patched in Damion, Skid, and Wild Bill. I spent a lot of time with Damian and Skid as prospects. I wouldn't have missed it for the world. Wild Bill would later take a beating from me and be tossed from the club. More on that later.

Damian and Skid would give me some of the greatest memories in this club. We had some wild times. From the road cone walk of shame Damian stopped as the fun police in Bergen to Skid, Craig, and I banging out half the women that lived in their complex in one weekend! Damian and I would go on working together on many different levels, trying to do the right thing for the club. He served as my national vice president for my first term as national president. The Marine Corps ruled for that year. Semper Fi! Much love and respect to those brothers.

I hooked Jay up with a broad I knew in Savannah. Then we rode over to Gainesville, Georgia, to visit the North Georgia chapter for their first ever "open house." There I got a threesome lined up for Little Billy.

On the way home, we stopped in Roanoke to visit Kim, Dani, and Mary. I know how to set the hook! When we left Virginia in the morning, I thought, *Let me see what these guys got for riding legs*, and decided to let loose for a while on Route 81 north and see if they could keep up. Well, we were ripping it. Weaving and blocking for each other. It was like we had been riding together for years. Then Little Billy cut into the left lane and brake checked a car for Jay and I to get in the lane. Then I saw the lights and heard the siren. It was an unmarked car!

We pulled over, and I told them, "Let me talk. Don't say a word!"

This trooper was like seventy years old and pissed. I started walking toward him, and he screamed, "Don't take another step." He then pointed at Jay and said, "You get the fuck out of here!"

I nodded to Jay, and he rode about a half mile up the road. Then he turned to me and said, "Stay right there. I'm not sure if you're going to jail yet!" Then it was little Billy's turn. "You, you little fuck, get in the back seat of my car. You are definitely going to jail!"

He cuffed Billy then came to me and just started reaming me out. I mean he was bumping my face with the brim of his Smokey Bear cover and spraying my face with his enraged shouting. I had flashbacks of boot camp and was standing locked up fingernails on seams on the side of the road. His breath stunk of coffee and ciga-rettes. He finally stopped screaming.

I said, "Sir, you're right. We were riding like assholes, but they were following me and my direction. If you're going to lock someone up, let it be me and not them."

He went into drill-instructor mode again and started scream-ing, "Why are you not arguing back?"

I told him, "It's kind of hard to argue when I know we were riding like idiots on a death wish."

Well, he wasn't done screaming, then he started explaining how they just "scrapped" a guy off the pavement two days ago, and on and on he went.

Finally, I said, "Sir, either arrest me or please stop screaming in my face."

He got right in my face and said, "I know my breath stinks. My wife complains all the time!"

Now I was starting to think maybe we were on some prank TV show and a camera crew was going to jump out. He went in the car and was in the front seat, screaming at Billy now. Then all of a sudden, he got out and got Billy out, uncuffed him, got back in his car, and left.

Billy was literally hyperventilating. He begged me to let him smoke a cigarette. Jay rode down the shoulder to us and said, "So, yeah, what do I have to do to become a Wingmen?" I will never understand why he let us go. Billy and Jay both stood up that follow-ing weekend and started prospecting.

August 8, 2009. Bergen rode up to Orange County for the last party to be held there. It sucked to know we wouldn't be going there anymore, but we adapt and overcome. We had some great times in that house for sure. I did a major amount of my prospecting time in that house. I formed and bonded brotherhood and friendships that I know will last a lifetime in that house.

That night was a blur. Everyone from Bergen, Rockland, and Orange were there, as well as a few out-of-state brothers. I remember a big bonfire. I remember waking up in Ed's camper. Pretty much that was it.

I had reached fifty thousand club miles on the ride home that Sunday. Not bad for a year and nine months as a patch holder. I was killing Ms. Bettie though. I don't remember the exact dates, but she had three motor replacements and one tranny rebuild and a tranny and primary replacement as well. I have since sold her to brother Albie in 2021, with the agreement she always stays in the club. I don't really ride her anymore, and he needed a bike. She had 206,000 and change on her at the time and still runs great. If you buy a new bike and plan on banging out miles, buy the warranty. Worth its weight in gold.

August 12, 2009. Myself and Lil Billy headed out to Oak Grove for the pistol shoot. On the way, we ran over to Kernersville to hook up with my civilian friend, James. We crashed at his house, and the next day, we went fishing and shooting guns and shit. We headed out the next day for Kentucky.

Roy Willey had brought his .50 caliber rifle to Oak Grove, and we were blowing shit up all weekend. Roy always has had a collection fit to defend a small country. I remember it being balls hot as usual in Kentucky that time of year. That Saturday Karate Joe from Rockland and I had bought, like, fifty bags of ice and strung a bunch of those kid's pool noodles together to form a barrier in the pool filled with the ice. We sat there drinking all day and never left the pool.

August 16, 2009. Got one of the worst phone calls ever in my life this day. Got the call our brother Curtis Jeffs from Rockland County had passed on and joined the Gone but Not Forgotten chapter.

Cannot say enough good things about Curtis. He was Wingmen through and through. Curtis had come to me a few weeks before at an open house in Bergen and handed me an envelope of money. He said he wanted Bergen to have it to help out with our bills. I knew then Curtis knew something and wasn't wanting to talk about it. Curtis again was and always will be remembered as a great man and a great Wingmen.

August 19–20, 2009. Attended Curtis's wake and funeral. A ton of brothers showed up on a short funeral schedule to see our beloved brother off to the Gone but Not Forgotten chapter. Many, many great times and one road trip I'll never forget. Brother, I am thankful to God I got to share time with you on this earth. See you when it's my time, brother. Love ya.

August 28, 2009. I headed to Savannah and had my Virginia friend, Kim, meet me there. She was in town for some work convention. Then I headed over to Beaufort to hang out with Skid and Craig. Skid, Craig, and I were day drinking at the pool then hit a few bars that night. I woke up in a dorm room with two girls that, combined, didn't make up my age. I remember waking up and opening my eyes and seeing a poster of Michael Jackson staring at me on the ceiling. I met Craig and Skid at an IHOP, and I was in pretty bad shape. I had promised Calhoun County I would meet up with them in Calhoun along with Roy Willey to ride back to Fayetteville with them for nationals.

I remember getting eyeballed by a cop in the IHOP because I walked in with a pint bottle of Jack in my hand, and I was visibly drunk. Skid and Craig were trying to talk me out of riding to Calhoun. I told them, "I gave my word. I'll be okay." Well, I did make it in the middle of the night. I showered and racked out.

The next morning, I heard a bunch of bikes and cages coming into the parking lot, and I got up and opened the door to see the brothers and some ole ladies and civilians congregating for the trip.

That's when I saw her. She was getting out of her car and walked over to Chief and Katrina. She was beautiful, blond hair, blue eyes, great smile. But what was different was, I wasn't saying to myself, *I want to bang this broad.* I said to myself, *I need to get to know her.* I walked over to say hello, and my friend Rhonda came running over and jumped on my back to hug me and say hello. Well, unbeknownst to me, while Rhonda and I were saying hello, this woman asked Katrina who I was. Now Katrina loves me as I her, but she also knows me. She just looked at her and said, "*No,* not Butta, please not Butta!"

I walked over, and I hugged Chief and Katrina, then I extended my hand and said, "Hey. I'm Butta. I don't think we've met."

She shook my hand and said, "Hello. I'm Heather." She had me at hello.

We saddled up, and Roy and I were leading the pack. At the first gas stop, I went to Heather's car and asked if Katrina would drive so Heather could get on the back of Miss Bettie. She (Katrina) reluctantly agreed. She rode with me to south of the border, South Carolina. I walked her back to her car and asked if she would spend the weekend with me. She said yes.

Heather and I spent every moment we could together that weekend. I called Lucille and told her what was going on so as not to get her sideswiped by the phone calls from old ladies there that can't mind their own business.

She headed for Alabama that Sunday morning, and I headed to New Jersey. That would be happening a lot over the next year.

I will get this out of the way now. Though Heather will be in some of the travel stories to follow, I'll explain our destiny in one shot.

CHAPTER 10

Heather

Heather and I were in love at hello. Yeah, break my balls and say I'm a pussy, but it's true. She changed my life, and I like to think I changed hers. I could never be in a relationship in my lifetime up till then. I trusted no woman no matter how good they were to me, or how hard I tried. My ex-wife, Lucille, is a great person and loved me and never did anything to make me feel otherwise. She was a great wife, and I was a horrible husband, plain and simple.

I was very self-centered and selfish back then. It was all about me period. Now, to my defense, I also let anyone trying to get into my life know exactly how I was. I hid nothing from no one. Any woman in my life chose to be there knowing full well what I was about.

My life was in this order: my club, me, my kids, then whoever wanted to accept that. Not saying it was the right way to be, but that was me for a really long time.

I could never be as happy with my wife, Jill, and love and trust her the way I do now if I didn't learn from Heather how to truly let myself love and trust a woman. She single-handedly transformed me.

On April 14, 2010, Heather and I were in Savannah. I was national SAA then, and Lee had a meeting with a club. Heather and I were going to the pimp and hoe party in Long County afterward. That morning she woke up, and her eye was bloodshot, and we had thought she got something in it and maybe scratched her cornea or something.

Well, a few months or so later, we would find out she had T-cell lymphoma, and her eye had a tumor behind it. She would seek treatment at the University of Alabama Spain-Wallace Building in Birmingham, Alabama. We had a rough couple of months between the distance, her family (which did not approve of our relationship) and her thinking it was better if I moved on due to her illness.

But her family gave in a little, and I was able to get extended time off work, and I spent a few days here and there at the hospital. Her condition wasn't improving nor was it degrading at the time. One doctor recommended chemo and radiation, and one recommended bone marrow transplant. Heather didn't like the attitude of the second doctor, and though myself and her mom wanted her to go with the transplant, she chose the chemo and radiation.

She didn't like him because he was honest, to the point, and blunt. She wasn't going to survive this cancer, and he was clear about that. He did tell her though, if she listened to him, he could get her probably about five years of a good quality of life if she got the transplant. The first doctor was the complete opposite and swore that chemo and radiation would cure her. I went home to work for a couple of weeks and returned to the hospital on August 29, 2010.

The hospital staff were great. We had a room next to hers set up for her mom when I visited, and they put a second bed next to Heather's so we were able to sleep next to each other.

September 4 was our national meeting in Calhoun. I remember Heather asking me not to go. I was a national officer, and though I know my brothers would've understood if I didn't attend, it's just not me. I had a job to do, and I was going to do it. We had a big meeting set up for 1700 hours that night after the national meeting. One of our chapters got into it with another club, and we had around ten or so brothers arrested a few weeks prior to the national meeting. We had some things to discuss and needed to get the full story of what went down. I told Heather I would be there before they lock the building down. Well, brother Chopper was our national vice president then and was running on Chopper time as usual. At around

1745, Lee told me to take off and go to the hospital. Once again, it was my responsibility to be there; I'd see it through. Well, by the time Chopper arrived and we started, the meeting didn't end till around midnight. I jumped on my bike, and I headed to Birmingham. But as expected, the building was closed down, and I slept in a booth at a twenty-four-hour McDonald's.

Heather was pissed, but she understood my commitment to the club. Her mother was a different story. She ripped into me pretty good in the hallway before I got in the room to see Heather. That day we spent together just going through pictures on our phones and reminiscing of all the trips we took. The next morning, I headed for home again. Heather was getting a treatment done that was going to put her in a coma and have a chemo treatment with a chemo that was still experiential, and within two weeks, she was to either wake up and they would be able to measure the success of the treatment or she wouldn't awake at all.

I returned home to work and see my kids. I kept a bag packed in my trunk as to be able to leave as soon as I got the call that she was waking up. I spoke with her mom several times a day on her condition.

September 20, 2010. I got the call from her mom that she was waking up and I needed to get there as soon as I could. It is minimum fourteen hours from Jersey to Birmingham booking it. I jumped in my little Kia Rio and hit the pavement from work. Around 2200 hours, I knew something was wrong. Her mom hadn't called, and last I heard, I just needed to hurry. Around 2330 Chief called me and told me things weren't good. She had awoken, but she was having heart attacks and having to be revived. He said they were trying to keep her alive long enough for me to get there. I told Chief to tell her family not to do that and just let what happens happen; it was in God's hands now.

A few hours later, I think it was around 0130 hours on the twenty-first, just as I hit the Alabama state line, Chief called to let me know Heather had passed. I said thank-you and to let her mom know I would be there in a few hours. I pulled over and really didn't know what to do. I was pretty numb. I called my friend Aimee and broke down. I got back on the road, and then my brother Ian called. Gotta be honest, if not for that call, I don't know what I would've done. The pain was immeasurable.

I got to the Spain-Wallace Building before dawn. It was locked down, and I didn't know what to do. I saw an old Black man who was a security guard in the parking garage and told him my situation. He came out of his booth and gave me an embrace I'll never forget. He truly felt and understood my pain. He made a few phone calls, and a few minutes later, a woman came to replace him in the booth, and he brought to an elevator and up to Heather's floor. He again embraced me and said a prayer for us.

The nurses were expecting me and, they kept Heather there till I arrived. I got my closure and got to say goodbye.

The staff at University of Alabama Spain-Wallace are among the best people I have ever met. Every one of them. They truly understand what families are going through.

I left the hospital and went to my brother Redneck's house to cut his three acres or so of grass with his tractor. I really wasn't out of the shock yet, and I figured, if I kept busy, it would be better. Redneck and Miss Arlene loved Heather, and I felt it was the right place to be. Redneck had had a stroke a while back in New Jersey and was bedridden (more on that later). I then went to a brother Ron Harris's house, and he and his wife, Misti, let me stay there for the week till Heather's funeral.

Heather's parents and I had a long talk, and I think they might have finally understood the relationship her and I had. Gotta remember they were born and raised in the Bible belt of Alabama. I was an older married guy with four kids from New Jersey who met their daughter through mutual friends in a motorcycle club.

Didn't make it any easier for them to swallow, but they did know and acknowledge I made her the happiest they had ever seen her, and they knew she loved me. That's all that mattered to me. They included me as family for her wake and funeral.

I could never repay Heather for showing me how to accept someone's unconditional love or how to return it. It is because of her I learned how to love unconditionally and what to look for in the person to accept it from. It is because of our relationship then I am so in love and happy now with Jill.

That is the story of Heather for those who didn't know what really happened. I am a pretty personable guy, and I don't put my life on Facebook. At least not the attention-seeking stuff. There is a picture that hangs in the North Georgia clubhouse of Heather and I. That is my favorite picture of us. Brother Halfway put it up after she passed. North Georgia was her favorite clubhouse to visit.

I think back often on the day and night of that national meeting. I could've had one more day and night with her. Don't ever doubt my commitment to this club or my duties. Ever.

So back to the trips. August 28, 2009 through September 6, 2009 trip just explained. Visited Savannah, Beaufort, P Cal, Opelika, Calhoun, and Fayetteville. Road a total of 2,730 miles that week. Met Heather.

September 10, 2009. The following week, I headed to Calhoun for their anniversary party. Heather and I jumped on Miss Bettie, and she showed me all the cool stuff in Calhoun County. We went to Talladega speedway, Mount Cheaha, and just riding around. The small town of Oxford, Alabama, would be my second home for the next year. The Calhoun chapter almost gave me a bottom rocker to change over to.

September 18, 2009. I was back in Dirty Jersey, and myself, Tiny, Charlie Balls, Frankie the Elbow, and prospects Al and Lil Billy took a brother by the name of "Wild Bill" over to players strip club. This guy was a tool. He got sideways puking drunk within an hour. We had to take him out of the bar. He was so belligerent to everyone. Finally, Charlie Balls just dropped him then looked at me and said, "I know it is your job, but Christ, I just couldn't take it anymore!"

Bill, as you may have guessed, is no longer in the club either. Another example of a guy who just goes to asshole mode after patching out. He was later tuned up by myself and tossed due to some shit he and his daughter tried to drag a brother into.

October 7, 2009. Headed to Heather's again this time for a ten-day trip. We rode to Devil's Elbow for their anniversary party. I remember Luis from Beaufort was a prospect for that party. I also remember saying to myself I'd never seen a happier prospect. Nothing could take the smile from that soon-to-be brother's face.

I headed back to New Jersey on the fifteenth, and it was around thirty-eight degrees and rain the whole way. Can't have the sun on your head the whole time, I guess.

October 16, 2009. Great night. One of my favorite brothers and by far the club's best cook, Al, was patched in Bergen. Al has been a constant solid brother for our chapter and for the nation.

October 17, 2009. Myself, prospects Lil Billy and Jay went to a local club's party. They are for the most part a good bunch of guys but have a few undesirable, weak-ass pussies as well. One of them is an acquaintance of one of my Bergen brothers, and I can't stand him. He is always joking and is never serious.

Well, I happen to be talking to one of the area's 1 percent club members inside, with Billy and Jay flanking my rear. All of a sudden, I felt like someone bumped into me, and I didn't really pay it any mind. Then all of a sudden, I distinctly felt someone kick me in the ass. I turned around, and it was this moron. He was shit-faced and thought it was funny. I looked at Jay and Billy and asked them, "Why are you not smashing his head in?" They both looked at each other then back at me like they didn't have a clue. I stepped into this guy and hit him square across his throat with my forearm. He went flying into the drummer of the band.

I looked at Jay and Billy and told them they had better get involved soon, or they were next. They jumped on him and started dragging him out the back door. Now, mind you, this was happening in his house, not mine. I turned to the 1 percent member I was talking to and said, "I'll see you soon," and shook his hand and went out the back door.

I went outside, and Jay and Billy got this idiot by the arms. His president ran outside (still, not one of his brothers stood up to us for him) and started pleading with me not to continue. I called off Jay and Billy, and president and I walked behind a truck to talk. I told him this guy was a moron and what he was doing. He assured me he would talk to him. I told him if it happened again with this guy, it was going to be a broader issue. Not one of their patches did a fucking thing; well, they did buy us beers after that.

October 6, 2009, I headed to Alabama to see Heather, then her and I, along with some Calhoun brothers, were heading to North Georgia for their twenty-second anniversary party. Little Kenny, along with prospects Jay and Lil Billy, met me in North Georgia. We had a great time; I can't remember for sure, but I think that was the time I beat up the drummer for taking a swing at brother Stew, who was breaking up another fight.

Heather got a ride home with Katrina. Myself, Kenny, Jay, and Billy headed out at zero dark thirty. I remember we got lost 'cause Kenny got a "new route" from a North Georgia brother. Remember, pre-GPS on bike days. So we were lost, and the fog was intense I remember that real heavy, wet fog. I was riding front right when, all of a sudden, Kenny kicked me in the thigh. He didn't try to explain, just looking straight ahead and riding. We spotted a McDonald's and pulled in to eat.

I parked and said, "What the fuck did you kick me for?"

Now, those that know Kenny, he never changes his tone or gets worked up. Everything is just kind of "matter-of-factly" with him.

He simply turned to me and said, "Bro, you were out cold. I let you go for a mile or so, then you started veering off, so I kicked you to wake you up."

Got to love that brother right there.

October 16, 2009. Heather got on a plane and headed to New Jersey for a week. We would go to New York City and do some tourist stuff then end the week at Bergen County's Halloween party.

I picked her up at Newark Airport. Heather had never really been out of Alabama except to Georgia and Florida. So the look on her face when she saw the famous New York skyline for the first time was priceless.

The next day, we went riding in the city. We went over the George Washington Bridge then down the West Side Highway. Went to Times Square and hit a street fair in the Village. It was a great day. I sometimes forget the magic of the city, since living five minutes away and growing up going there all the time desensitizes the magnitude of the place. But I am reminded of its magic when I bring someone there that is a New York City virgin.

We ate pizza in the Village and had desserts at Rocco's Café on Bleecker Street. Went to the World Trade Center and then back up to Central Park. We took the Lincoln Tunnel back to Dirty Jersey, and the rest of the week we just chilled with brothers and did some more sightseeing stuff.

October 23, 2009. Bergen's Halloween party. We threw one of the area's best Halloween parties. The place was packed, and all were enjoying themselves. A brother and his ole lady from Calhoun County attended, Redneck and Miss Arlene. Redneck was a very quiet brother. Not loud or obnoxious in any way. His ole lady was originally from Staten Island. Her and I would always talk about the East Coast when I was in Alabama. She used to own a bar on the docks where a lot of Merchant Marines and dock workers frequented. That is where she met our brother, Redneck, who was a Merchant Marine at the time. They fell in love, and when he retired, she sold the bar, but not the building, and they moved to his native Alabama. They bought an incredible plot of land in Central Alabama. Twenty-plus acres with a big-ass pond filled with giant catfish. About one third of the property was cleared and only grass. Redneck used to let me drive his tractor and mow the lawn every time I went there. Love and miss you both, brother.

Well, around seven o'clock the next morning, my phone was blowing up. Apparently, Redneck stayed at the clubhouse to party while Miss Arlene went back to the hotel. Early the next morning, he was unresponsive when brothers were trying to wake him up 'cause Miss Arlene had showed up to get him. He had a massive stroke during the night. He was rushed to the hospital and survived.

However, a few days later, the doctors would try to convince Miss Arlene to pull the plug, citing he would never leave a hospital bed or be able to really communicate or be physically able to leave a bed.

She would have nothing to do with it, and he ended up in New Jersey for about three months before being strong enough to move him back to Alabama.

I remember one day Frankie the Elbow went to sit with them (Bergen sent one brother just about every day to visit and see if Miss Arlene needed anything). Well, Frank called me and said, "You have to get here pronto." I asked what was up, and he didn't want to talk about it on the phone. I headed over, and he met me in the hallway to tell me he was pretty sure Miss Arlene's handbag had a gun in it. Now, I know all my Southern brothers are right now thinking, *So?* Well, this is the Northeast Communist Bloc of the United States of America, folks. You could go to jail for a paper clip if it has a sharp edge on it.

I went in the room and gave her a hug and kissed my brother. I asked Miss Arlene to talk to me outside the room. I asked her if she had a gun in her bag, and she was like, "Of course, I do. I don't go anywhere without my guns." I tried to explain to her that this was New Jersey, and you could be locked up pretty much just for the bullets. Well, I grabbed her handbag and headed out to my bike. I went to the clubhouse to secure the gun. Well, it wasn't a gun. It was guns—plural! She had three handguns and two sets of brass knuckles in her bag!

I have to say, I wish she would've listened to the doctors 'cause, till his death, he never left the bed unless put in a wheelchair and could never speak or have any control over his limbs again. I understand her not wanting to let go, but no one should live that way in my eyes. I visited them often even after Heather passed. Redneck did know me when I would visit. I remember I would enter his home and scream at the top of my lungs, "ALAMUTHERFUCKINGBAMA," and he would try his hardest to scream it back to me.

Miss Arlene ended up passing in 2018, and our Brother Redneck passed August 5, 2019. I miss them both terribly. Love you, brother.

That ride concludes any relevant rides for 2009. I rode 20,829 club miles, hitting my goal of 20,000. I visited out-of-state chapters twenty-nine times that year. I was awarded my second Captain Wingmen Award for that year.

CHAPTER 11

2010: My Goal Was to Ride Twenty-Five Thousand Miles for This Year

December 30, 10. Myself, Chaz, Little Kenny, and Johhny Crash jumped in my Kia Rio and headed to Oak Grove for winter nationals. Now, that's a lot of meat in a small container, but the Rio got almost forty miles a gallon, and New Jersey and New York were covered in snow and ice.

Our first gas stop was in Pennsylvania somewhere. We all piled out, went and hit the head, and grabbed some snacks and shit. Well, this station had a table selling some local beef jerky. Myself and Kenny grabbed some. Well, Chaz started telling us we were crazy, eating some local shit we didn't know, what's in it, la la la la la… Real mother-hen shit. He meanwhile grabbed the $9 a bag of Jack Link's for himself, saying, "This can be trusted over the homemade shit."

We pulled out of the gas station and got on the road. Chaz was driving now. Not three minutes in, we got lit up and pulled over. Now we were all sober, and as far as I know, no one took any kind of drugs. Well, Johhny Crash was in the front passenger seat and just started cracking up, yelling at Chaz, "Yo, Ace, you got lit up," over and over even while the trooper was asking Chaz for his paperwork. Now, I guarantee this trooper wasn't expecting us in that Kia Rio. He asked if we had been drinking, and Chaz said no while Johhny, myself, and Little Kenny were just cracking up. If you know Chaz, you'll understand the laughter.

The trooper was scared and had hand on gun the whole nine. He told Chaz he swerved and almost hit the trooper while we were getting on the interstate. Chaz told him it wasn't his car, first time driving it, and "it is like a fucking go-cart." Trooper just gave Chaz back his papers and said, "Be careful." All while Johhny was still screaming, "Yo, Ace, you got jacked," over and over.

Now we were cruising. We were eating beef jerky and drinking Red Bulls when, all of a sudden, Chaz pulled over abruptly and ran out to the back of the car without saying a word. We thought he had to pee. When we heard him retching his innards out from the bowels of hell! Now, again, you need to know Chaz to appreciate the situation. Chaz back then would've died for his vanity. Seriously, he would ride at night with the darkest sunglasses on because he looks cooler in them than clear or yellow ones. So here he was, retching and trying to stand straight up with his hands on his hips as to say, "Yeah, I'm puking, but I look cool doing so!" He got back in the car, and I said, "Funny how he is puking and we aren't. Maybe the big-corporation beef jerky wasn't such a good idea." He yelled at me to "shut up, the jerky had nothing to do with it."

Well, I think it was on the sixth or seventh time we had to pull over and watch Chaz heave on the side of the car when he finally said, "Okay, maybe it was the jerky!" Karma at its finest.

We got to Oak Grove; Heather met me there. We had a good meeting, and there was pretty good participation for a winter national in Kentucky. I received my second Captain Wingmen award for 2009. We made it home without incident!

February 25, 2010. I headed to Calhoun, and Heather and I went to stay with Redneck and Miss Arlene for a day and night. Heather would take Miss Arlene to get her hair and nails done and all the grocery shopping while I would sit and talk to our brother Redneck. Now, Redneck was quite aware of his surroundings. He understood what you would say and/or what was going on around him. He just had no way to communicate back except to nod yes or no. I cherished these visits with Redneck, plus I got to ride a tractor.

The next day, Heather and I headed to Phenix City for a dice run. Got to hang out with my brothers and have a good time and ride our bikes together. This was another one of those trips that made the money spent on heated gear worth it.

February 27, 2010. While I was gone, Bergen had a stag party. Jay was still a prospect. Remember Tiny I mentioned earlier? Well, he had always acted like an ass with prospects. It got to the point where Jay had to make a decision. Stand up like a man or risk the chapter seeing he will take any amount of abuse. I wasn't there due to me still being in Phenix City. But the story goes, Jay had had enough of Tiny's shit and called him out. Jay put the boots to him, and Tiny ended up quitting like a pussy.

March 10, 2010. I headed out to Calhoun again for a few days, then we headed to Savannah for their annual Saint Patty's Day party. A bunch of Bergen brothers caged down as well. Savannah has that holiday locked down tight. Seems everyone who lives there stops in the clubhouse that weekend. I remember a bunch of us being harassed by some local police down by the waterfront. Gotta love cops. They all want to be us on the weekends and play biker dress-up then do nothing but break our balls when they are on duty. Heather got a ride back to Calhoun with Katrina, and I rode home.

March 21, 2010. Due to an unfortunate event with our national sergeant of arms, Von Zipper, on this day, he was removed from the position, and Lee appointed me national sergeant of arms from regional sergeant of arms.

March 25, 2010. I headed down to Long County to stay with CC for a night, then we headed over to our North Georgia chapter for their annual swap meet.

We had received some intel that the local 1 percent club was going to show up in mass with support to our event. We weren't at odds with them and didn't take the intel as threatening, but we were prepared for any situation that may have arisen.

They showed up about twenty or so deep, with another twenty or so supporters in tow. I remember them thinking they weren't going to pay to get in. Well then, they got to the door and were greeted by our "little angry Mexican, Mr. Jack Backer." Jack politely told them they didn't have to pay; they can just turn around and hang out in the parking lot and/or leave. There were some angry stares and a lot of whispering in ears because they weren't used to this at all and really didn't know how to handle the situation. Finally, one of their national officers who was with them said, "Either pay to get in or wait outside. I'm paying and going in."

I will never forget the looks on their faces as they handed over $10 each and were greeted by Jack shaking their hand and saying, "Thank you for supporting the Wingmen nation. Have a great day!" He did that to every one of them that entered!

April 14, 2010. I headed to Calhoun. Heather and I went and stayed a few days with Miss Arlene and Redneck. Did the usual. Heather took Miss Arlene to do girlie stuff and grocery shopping, etc. I wheeled Redneck outside, and he watched me mow his acres of grass, wash his bikes, and do some catfishing.

Morning of the sixteenth, Heather and I jumped on Ms. Bettie and headed to Atlanta to hook up with Uncle Billy. We rode to Macon, Georgia, and met with Roy and his ole lady and proceeded to Long County. That ride I wanted to kill Roy. He took us through all back roads covered in gravel, and it was typical Georgia furnace weather already even though it was only April. For those that don't know, I hate any temperature over sixty degrees! It felt like it took us two days to get to Long County.

The next day, I headed over to Savannah (Uncle Billy, Roy, and Heather would meet me there later in the day). Myself and Lee had a meeting with a local club from the Florida–Georgia border. I rode to Savannah and let myself in using a key Buzz had left me in a hidden spot. Now I was sweating like a pig already in the ungodly Georgia heat. So I decided to take a shower. Now, I am very sensitive about my height. I know I'm not the shortest guy, but I don't like only being five feet seven inches first thing in the morning. I remember going in to take a shower and getting so pissed off because I had to get a Spackle bucket to move the fucking showerhead that Roundy put, like, nine feet in the air! The frigging water knobs were eye level!

Needless to say, that put me in a mood to begin with, then throw in the heat. It was safe to say I wasn't in a jovial mood. These guys showed up, and we were all at the bar as some Savannah brothers were still showing up. Now, some of our Savannah brothers are very big (both tall and dense). I remember every time a brother showed, these guys got more and more nervous. Finally, everyone that was supposed to be there was, and we adjourned to the meeting room. I just got the feeling one of them was a cop. I asked Lee if I could just smash him. We knew he was lying, and he just gave off a very shady demeanor. Lee told me to stand down unless he gave me the nod.

Well, this guy pretty much caved in the meeting, and an agreement was met. I was even more pissed now because I never got the nod.

We were all at the bar, having a customary after-meeting drink, when this douche I believed to be a cop came up and said, "Man, I was kind of happy you were here."

I looked at him and asked, "Why would that be?"

He said, "Well, look at the size of some of these guys. It was nice to see someone under six feet in the room."

Yeah, I blew a gasket. I grabbed him by the throat had him up against the bar and was shouting, "Do you know who the fuck I am? I'll fucking kill you!"

I got pulled off him. They left, and we never saw their patch again. We did confirm he was a cop a while later as well.

Heather, Roy, and Uncle Billy showed up, and we hung out downtown Savannah for some pizza and sightseeing. We then headed back to Long County for the pimp and hoe ball, where I believe that was the year that "Roid Willey" won pimp of the year!

That night Roy, CC, and myself were talking about the Opelika anniversary party the following weekend. I told them I needed a break and was going to stay home that weekend. Roy said he would ride up to New Jersey to personally escort me to the event.

Now, you have to consider, when I return to New Jersey from this trip, it will be a total of almost 2,500 miles. Going to Opelika and back will be another two-thousand-plus miles. I was tired, and so was Ms. Bettie. Then CC upped the ante and also agreed to come to New Jersey with Roy.

April 20, 2010. Needless to say, Myself, CC, PD (CC talked him into coming as well), and Roy departed New Jersey en route to Calhoun to get Heather and then hit Opelika for their anniversary party.

On the way down, we decided to stop in Carlisle, Pennsylvania, to have lunch with our brother OB who was working at the war college for a while. We had a great time and went to this little German pub. Then PD got this like six-inch spike in the sidewall of his tire and lost an exhaust bracket. I didn't think we were going to make it.

We had a great time in Opelika. Man, I miss that old clubhouse. It had some character to it. I dropped off Heather and headed home in a wicked rainstorm, ending another two-thousand-plus-mile, five-day weekend.

May 22, 2010. I was heading out on another ten or so day tour. First stop was in Fayetteville. Then I headed down to Beaufort to hang out with the Marines for a bit. I then headed over to Calhoun to pick up Heather and meet up with a bunch of brothers I had planned a trip with. The plan was to head to Tunica, Mississippi, to go to the Hollywood Casino then push on to Devil's Elbow for nationals.

Myself, CC, PD, Fat Mike, Country, Dirty Dick Dino, and Chopper met me in Calhoun. That afternoon myself, CC, PD, Ron, Ghangis, and Chief were hanging out at the clubhouse. A car came pulling in, and some guy in a suit with a briefcase came up and asked to speak to the owner of the establishment. The clubhouse used to be an old warehouse. It had a loading dock with trailer slips and all. So I could see his thinking it was a business.

Ron let him know it was a motorcycle clubhouse and not a place of business, and the guy apologized and started heading back to his car. I asked him who he was. He stopped and turned and extended his hand and introduced himself as a district judge who was running for state senate. Me being a ball-breaker and all decided to remind him that bikers do vote and asked if he wanted a beer and shoot us his pitch. He refused the beer but decided to come inside and give his pitch to the Alabama brothers.

Well, he was going on and on, and finally he got to gun control. He started in with how guns are bad, etc. I interrupted him and said, "Oh, you must be a Democrat." He replied that he was. We all laughed and made a few jokes. He then looked around and said with a twinge of sarcasm in his voice, "This is a really big place with a big piece of property. How do you guys pay for all this?" Well, what happens next is an illness of mine that happens every so often when my quick-witted thinking and unfiltered mouth come together for an epic response. I just blurt out, "We are a motorcycle club. We sell meth to pay the bills. Why? What were you thinking?" Well, you could tell he knew I was busting balls, but brothers Ron and CC lost it. They went into full damage-control mode and were rattling off how I was from New Jersey and just joking, and we are a military club, and no one does drugs, etc. I never laughed so hard in my life. CC laid into me for a few days for that one.

After that all the other brothers slowly showed up, and well, we did have to wait on Chopper and chopper time. Then Fat Mike said we needed to go through South Memphis to hit a barbecue place named Corky's he saw on some television food show. After some arguing and planning, we head for Memphis.

Now, South Memphis is really no place for White guys on motorcycles, and I pointed that out. We got into town and were stuck at a railroad crossing. Actually, we were aimlessly riding around South Memphis, looking for this place. Fat Mike wasn't the best road captain. Well, at the tracks, we saw a bunch of Black gangbangers coming out of what seemed to be projects. Next thing you know, they pulled guns, we pulled guns, and as Aldo Raines would say, "Seems we have ourselves a Mexican standoff." We explained we were just looking for Corky's, and one of them said his auntie worked there, and we followed him to the joint.

So we got there, and we ordered; and for the first time on this trip, we all agreed on something. The food sucked. I've had better barbecue in Hackensack, New Jersey! I did pocket a nice steak knife, which I still have and use.

We got rooms for the night, and we all hit Tunica early afternoon the next day. We checked into the casino and got cleaned up then met for dinner and a night of drinking and gambling. I believe PD hit for a decent amount on a slot machine. I remember Heather hit for $700 on the wheel of fortune slot.

The next morning, we waited in the parking lot for over an hour on Chopper time. What else was new. We made it to Devil's Elbow late afternoon. That was my first national as national sergeant of arms.

I went back to Heather's for a few days and then headed back home to Dirty Jersey. That trip was a little under 4,500 miles total.

June 24, 2010. I headed to Fayetteville to hook up with CC and most of our brothers from our North Carolina chapters. We all headed to the Smoke Out in Rockingham. We were actively seeking to claim Rockingham for a chapter then.

I remember walking around with Lee and Albie. We stopped by the dominant 1 percent club's swag tent to shoot the shit with their local president. He and Lee went back a long way. I ran into an old friend of mine, Miss Vicki, from Blackburn, Virginia. I remember her and I were off to the side, talking, when the 1 percent president and Lee came over. He and I exchanged greetings. Then a couple of brothers of ours from our Little River chapter came walking by Randy (Daddio) and Scotty to Hotti. The president waved to Randy and Scotty, and Randy replied, "Hey, Billy [not his real name]," and nodded. Then I noticed Scotty just walked by mean, mugging him.

That really chapped my ass, and I approached Scotty later in the day when I saw him. I asked him the reason for his actions. He replied, "Well, we don't support them." I then asked him if he thought it was a good idea to potentially put his national president, vice president, and sergeant at arms possibly in harm's way by his actions since we were surrounded by his members. He looked confused. My point being is, if a man treats you like a man and acknowledges you, why would you act like a dick? He acknowledged you, so be a man and return the respect!

Listen, I get it. We don't kiss anyone's ass and go running to shake hands and introduce ourselves. But if a member of another club, or any man for that matter, acknowledges you, then you should always return the respect. And for the record, Scotty didn't make it too much longer as a Wingmen.

We ended the night at our Moore County clubhouse, and then I hit the road Sunday morning to return home.

July 2, 2010. I headed to Dawson County for their Fourth of July party. Heather was meeting me there. There ended up being an incident in New Jersey with a bunch of members from local coalition clubs and Odd Todd, Jay, and Little Billy the night of the third.

Against Heather's wishes, I jumped on my bike the next morning and headed back to New Jersey to handle some business.

July 7, 2010. Bergen County was out actively seeking members of a specific club due to the events on the third of July. We hit a few bars and some bike night spots when I finally found one of the members of the club we were looking for.

I remember CC and Bernie from Devil's Elbow chapter were with us. They were up early for our chopper show. We entered the bar, I saw my mark, and then Al gave me the nod. He was talking to some broad. I walked up. He turned white and said, "Hey, Butta, what's going on?" I asked her to walk away and told him he needed to defend himself. He put his hands up, palms out, and started an attempt to plead. I threw a right elbow and knocked him clean off his feet and down a small flight of stairs. I jumped on top of him and grabbed him by his throat. He was semiconscious, and I told him to look at me. I told him, "If you ever disrespect one of my brothers or my club again, I will cut you into little pieces and mail you all over the county." He started to say it wasn't him, and I gave him a short right hand to his left eye. Night night. I then got out of there with Frankie the Elbow.

I remember having to lay low for a few days because he was admitted to the hospital with bleeding on the brain and a broken orbital socket. He did the right thing. When asked what happened, he told police he tripped and fell down the steps. He still has a scar under his left eye of the Long County bottom rocker from my ring.

The next few days were funny. A lot of clubs reached out and asked the question, "Are we good?" We would just tell them, "As long as you don't disrespect us, all is good."

I got the call from their "landlord" the next day. They asked if I would sit with one of them and tell them "our side of the story." I met with a member I knew well, and we both have mutual respect for each other. I asked him what story he got from them. I didn't find out till later on that night that there was another one of the guy I smashed brothers in the bar. When we posted up in the bar, CC covered on him. He was sitting on a bench. When I cracked the guy, CC told the dude, "If you get up, you'll get fucked up." The dude sat and watched his brother get churched up. Well, that dude told a story like this. We (Wingmen) rolled in fifteen deep with bats, and he did his best to defend his brother and took a beating himself with baseball bats. Apparently, he had someone Dirty Harry him to make it look like he took a beating from us!

I looked at Jimmy (not his real name) and asked if that sounded like us. I told him we were five or so deep with no weapons. I told him to check with the bar. The place was packed, and I'm sure some-one would (if they hadn't already) run their mouth willingly. We were outside on the back deck. He knew our story over theirs was more likely the truth.

Dirty Harry dude ended up getting lumped up by the landlord and then his own club and sent packing. We haven't had an inci-dent with another club in Bergen since. Like the old saying goes: "Everyone's a tough guy till they get punched in the face."

July 10, 2010. Brothers started showing up to Bergen for our annual chopper show. If you haven't been to one, you need to attend one. Al puts out a spread all weekend long, and you would think you were on a buffet line for all the high-end Italian restaurants in the area. He goes all-out above and beyond.

Darren always makes a really cool trophy for the winners, and all in all, it is a really great weekend. The Saturday morning of the event, I take brothers and whoever else wants to go on a ride to show the brothers our AO and to show everyone in our AO just how big and widespread we are.

This weekend was special though. We patched out Jay that Friday night. It was great because he got to have a bunch of out-of-state brothers share the night with him. Jay worked long and hard for it and would go on to be our chapter president for a while and a cornerstone of our chapter.

Jay and I had a real love-hate relationship. He was an awesome brother, fun as fuck, but at times you just wanted to smash him because he was relentless at times and wouldn't let certain shit go. Jay and I rode thousands and thousands of miles together.

July 22, 2010. Myself and Lil Billy headed down to Fayetteville. We would link up with Jay, who was already down there; he went to visit family in Virginia, I believe. Once there, we linked up with Lee and Albie, and we all headed for Beaufort chapter for their annual Water Walk festival.

It's pretty cool, the main part of town with all the businesses, and all have a walkway behind them that meet up with the tidal pools and lagoons in the area. Some great restaurants and bars were visited.

Well, Jay decided he and another brother "Buckeye" from Calhoun County were going to see who can eat the most shrimp, and they planted their asses in this little seafood shack and just kept ordering shrimp by the bucket.

Well, the next morning we all got up and hit the road early to ride the seven-hundred-plus miles home. Jay wasn't looking so good. We had only gotten to south of the border on the 95 when we pulled over for fuel. Jay had his head in a trash can and was heaving. He ended up getting a room and staying there for two days till his shrimp attack stopped! Moral of the story: never try to outeat buckeye.

August 7, 2010. I headed to Calhoun 'cause Heather was sick. She was very lethargic and running a high fever for a few days. Her mother had finally talked her into going to the hospital. They admitted her, and no doctor could give an explanation of why she had these symptoms. Still no diagnosis. I stayed with her for two days while she ran crazy high fevers, then just like that, they stopped. The doctor did ask her to go to an optometrist specialist in Tennessee he recommended because her eye was still bothering her.

I returned home, and a few days later her, her mom and dad went to a specialist in Tennessee. That is when the word *cancer* first came into play. He had found a tumor behind her eye.

August 13, 2010. Johnny Law (Jag Lawyer in the USMC, not a cop) was now an active member of Bergen. He was in the process of leaving the Marine Corps and was planning on opening his own law firm. Johnny was dating this little hottie from his home state of Illinois, and she was flying in to spend some time with him. Now Rob Mas had just transferred to Bergen from Fayetteville as well. He was raised in Dirty Jersey, then the Army life took him all over the world.

Well, Jay, Lil Billy, Johnny, Rob, and I were going to get this broad at Newark Airport at, like, 1800 hours on our bikes. Johnny said, "Please don't ride crazy. She really isn't used to being on the back of a bike." Wrong thing to say. Just saying.

We were riding tight and on McCarter Highway in Downtown Newark traffic. I was front right. This immigrant in a beat-up minivan tried to slam her front end in front of Johnny, who was behind me. She readjusted and now moved forward and was trying to wedge in front of me. I just hauled off and started beating her driver's side window. I got it to spider up due to my rings, then she slammed on the accelerator and almost took me out, cut a few cars off to her right, and dee-deed out of sight. I looked at Rob and said, "Welcome home!"

We get to the airport, and Johnny got his toy on the back of the bike, and yes, as were all of Johnny's lady friends, she was a knockout in Daisy Dukes and cowboy boots. We started for home, and Jay and I decided to remind Rob what he moved away from and also scare the shit out of this broad. We were kicking it on Route 21, northbound, weaving and hitting the shoulder, the whole nine yards. When we got back to the clubhouse, our rotors were smoking. Rob was like, "Damn, I miss that shit," and Johnny started into like he was lead counselor in a triple homicide, and Rob, Billy, Jay, and I were the defendants. He finally stopped when he realized she loved it, and we probably warmed her up for later that night.

Later that night, No-Hurry Murry showed up, and he, Rob, and I decided to take a ride over to Lenora's Bar over in Hackensack and have a few cocktails. The joint was packed with twenty-something-year-olds. After a while of bullshitting with Lenora, I headed over to the head to take a piss, and there was someone just smashing this broad in the stall with the door closed. I was at the urinal, and this broad was just screaming all the typical porn lingo, and then I realized, I recognized those primal grunts and "yeah, take it, you fucking whore" comments. It's Murry in there, making new friends and spreading some love!

August 26, 2010. I headed to north Georgia then over to Dawson County for the patching of a prospect named Poppy. He and I spent a lot of time together during his prospecting time when I would travel south.

From Dawson, I rolled over to Calhoun County for their annual "Rumble on Noble" event. I met up with Jack Baker and CC for the day. Then I went to Birmingham to visit Heather, who had been admitted into the University of Alabama Spain-Wallace Building for cancer.

I then headed home and picked up my two youngest kids, Dominic and Melissa, and headed over to the Jersey Shore for a few days. That was a blast. Melissa was completely enthralled in the show, *Jersey Shore*, at the time. We actually got to meet them one early morning on the boardwalk. They were setting up at a pretzel stand to do a photo shoot. My daughter was about ten or eleven, and she had a crush on the kid Vinny from the show. I remember telling her to call him over and say hello to him. He was talking with one of the producers. She was shy and starstruck and couldn't speak a word, then the character Mike "the Situation" comes strolling over, trying to get Melissa to talk to him. She turned and looked at me and said, "Daddy, I don't like him." I looked at him and said, "Get the fuck outta here. My daughter doesn't like you." He was shocked and walked away. A state trooper then walked up to me and asked to shake my hand because he had never seen anyone speak to them that way.

Later that evening, we stood outside the *Jersey Shore* house, waiting for them to walk one hundred feet and get into a taxicab, but it was going to make my daughter really happy, so I stood there with her when about thirty seconds after, we got the signal that they were going to be coming out soon. Some photographer dude stepped in front of my daughter off the curb into the street. We were all told we couldn't stand in the street and had to stay on the curb.

I tapped him on the shoulder and said, "Hey, you're not planning on standing right there, are you?"

He looked back at me and said, "Yo, dude, I'm a professional photographer."

I looked at my daughter, and she knew what was coming next. I tapped him on the shoulder again, and I said, "Well, I am a professional asshole. If you don't move from in front of my daughter, I'm going to take your professional camera and shove it up your professional photographer's ass." He moved.

I dropped my kids off then headed out to Birmingham again to spend a few days with Heather. We celebrated our one-year anniversary in the hospital. I returned home on September 6, 2010 after the national meeting which I wrote about in chapter 10. I rode 4,803 miles from August 26 to September 6.

October 2, 2010. Al, Johnny Law, Lil Billy, and I rented a van and headed down to Long County. We had had a situation with another club in that area, and we were coming down for support, and we were coming down sterile; that is the reason for the van. Well, everything worked out. No one went to jail, and we had a great time. Saturday we all went and played paintball wars. Now this is probably the only time to date since I know CC that I have ever been fuming mad with him. We had selected teams, and it was basically all the guys from other chapters that showed up for support against the Long County chapter. Well, Long County had some dude hanging around at the time. I cannot remember his name, but he was like a professional paintball dude, and he had this paintball machine gun. No shit. So Johnny Law and I were running around in the woods when out of nowhere machine-gun dude stepped out from behind this tree and just started spraying us. There was this big, giant piece of plastic on the ground which looked to be an old side of a port-a-john. Johnny and I were fighting as hard as we could to make ourselves as small as we could and hide behind that piece of fucking plastic. It was pretty funny.

Well, I proceeded to get up and chase machine-gun dude, telling him I was going to fucking kill him. He ran to CC, and CC was like, "Bro, what's wrong?" And I'm like, "This motherfucker's got a machine gun," and machine-gun dude was like, "It's not a machine gun. I just have a really fast trigger finger." Well, that didn't help my current state of mind; in fact, it enraged me even more. CC sent machine-gun dude away, and he was trying not to laugh, and I was getting madder by the second. If you have never been hit with, like, fifty-two fucking paintballs in a row, then you can't understand my anger.

That finished up my memorable trips for 2010. I ended the year with 27,229 run miles. Attended fourteen national events, and I visited out-of-state chapters a total of twenty-nine times.

CHAPTER 12

2011

January 13, 2011. I headed out on my bike to Moore County for winter nationals. I was about two hours into the ride and freezing my ass off from the waist down before I realized I didn't plug in my heated pants to the jacket.

I remember the meeting, and all events at the club house were pretty normal, but the shenanigans at the hotel around the corner were off the chain. I remember pulling up the driveway to the hotel and seeing a bunch of brothers from Devil's Elbow, and their ole ladies had made a slip and slide on the front lawn. Yeah, it was, like, twenty degrees out, and they got a big sheet of plastic and mixed laundry detergent and water to cover it. Lots of naked bodies. Then I went inside, and a brother, Mark, from Phenix City is running around the hotel half naked with a four-foot fork. I didn't even want to know. I just went to my room and racked out.

On the ride home, I went out to Route 81 to avoid the tolls on the turnpike. Well, I got to Salem, Virginia, and it was four degrees out. I had to stop. Even the heated gear wasn't keeping me anywhere near warm. I got a room at a Haji motel and bedded down. Next morning, I got up. It was still just as cold. I said, *Fuck it. I have to get home.* Got all geared up, went out to start Bettie, and she was barely cranking due to the cold.

I decided to push her ass end into the room as far as I could get her. Pretty much right to the bars. I climbed over and into the room and stripped all the linens from the beds and took the pillows as well and started filling in the door space. I cranked the heat all the way up, got the blow-dryer from the bathroom, and started trying to get her motor warm enough to crank. About an hour or so later, I cranked her over, and she fired right up. Now she was still halfway in the room, and it was, like, 0500 hours! I threw all the linens and pillows on the bed, and I was gearing up again when Haji showed up, screaming at me about the noise and why the bike's ass end was in the motel, running yada, yada, yada. He wasn't happy, but I would be gone soon.

That was the coldest ride I have ever taken. It never went into double digits the whole way home. I remember getting in my Jacuzzi when I got home, and that fucking hurt so bad. I was in there for a few hours before I felt normal again.

January 20, 2011. So one week after almost freezing to death on my bike, what do I do? I rode to North Georgia and then onto Calhoun County! I went to go see my North Georgia brothers and then on to Alabama to see my brothers and to visit Heather's family and Redneck. Had a great time and was happy Heather's family didn't want to cut ties with me. The ride home, the weather was much more tolerable this trip than the one the week before.

February 19, 2011. Little Billy and I caged it down to Beaufort chapter. I had to handle some club business as the national sergeant at arms. We caged it due to snow up in New Jersey, and also, Billy didn't own any heated gear yet.

And for the guys reading this, saying, "Fucking pussy using heated gear!" Blah, blah, blah. These trips are ten-to-fifteen-hour trips. I don't care how much you layer up. If you're not generating heat, you won't go past four or five hours in less than thirty-five degrees. And if you can, good for you. I'll always use heated gear and be most of the time warm. Worth every penny if you ride all year round and live in the north.

Back to the trip. We had a guy named Wild Bill, the one I told you got knocked out up in Bergen a while back. Well, he was a weird dude for sure. He had gotten into some shit involving his stepdaughter (whom he pranced around like a hooker all the time) and a patch holder from another chapter. She made allegations against a brother that ended up being bullshit, and we had had enough. He had been asked in the past to keep her at bay, or at least on a leash.

So Wild Bill took a beating and was sent packing. That night I met Big Happy, one of my close brothers who was a prospect then. I remember sitting in the meeting room, getting to know him for a few hours after the night's events.

May 12, 2011. Little Billy and I headed to Calhoun for church that Friday night, then the chapter was throwing our brother Redneck a birthday party. We had a great time. We got Redneck into a wheelchair and strapped him in so he was outside all day, hanging out with us. I know he understood what was going on and who everyone was. We did some fishing, some shooting, and just had a great day among brothers and Redneck's family. Billy and I hit some serious rain just about the whole ride home that trip. I remember him at a gas stop saying, "Can't we just wait it out a while?" I told him, "If you wait, it may not stop. If we go, we may ride to the end of it." (No weather apps back then.) A lot of brothers don't like riding with me because I don't like to stop, even to eat. I always got something to pull out of my pockets or windshield bag to munch on. I want to get to where I'm going, and that is it.

May 23, 2011. I got a call that we lost a brother to a wreck from our Northeast Georgia chapter. His name is Tripp. Tripp and I were tight. We were also two polar opposites when it comes to where we lived and how we were brought up and so on. He was a backwoods country guy from the hills of Georgia, and I grew up fifteen minutes outside New York City. That's what I love about this club; it opens avenues to meet people I would never have thought I would have something in common with. I love my brother Tripp and miss him dearly. His wife gave me his Harley-Davidson hat he wore all the time. It is always in my saddle bag since I got it.

May 28, 2011. I may have this date screwed up, but not sure. I headed down to North Georgia to attend Tripp's funeral in Northeast Georgia that Sunday. From there I was going to head on over to Savannah for nationals the following weekend.

I was drinking whiskey in the North Georgia clubhouse that day and night. I can't stress it enough the way whiskey makes me do so really stupid shit. That afternoon I met Angela McIlvain. She is the widow of a brother, Voodoo Dave, who passed in March 2010. Voodoo was in retirement status and drove a truck across the country for a living. I never met him.

She and I were chatting on Facebook Messenger for a month or so. She reached out to me due to the common denominator of losing someone you loved. We finally met, and she planned on going to Savannah to hang out with me for national weekend. It would be the start of a near four-year thing.

That night I was pretty drunk, and around 0100 hours or so, a couple of very young strippers came down from the strip club at the top of the hill. One of them took a liking to me, and we ended up in the bunk room. I don't remember much of the night for real. I was really banged up. I was told she had gone to get the other stripper and went to the ladies' room, and then she came back to fall asleep. Jack Baker told me the next day her girlfriend told them I broke her.

The next morning, I'm panicking because I woke up, and this girl was lying naked on the floor next to my rack. She looked young, really young, and I was like, *What the fuck? I'm going to jail.* I walked out of the bunk room, and Jack was just coming in with McDonald's for everyone. I started screaming at him, "What the fuck, Jack? How could you let me do that? Why would you let her stay?" Etc. He looked at me and smiled and said, "Relax. She turned eighteen last week and just started stripped at the top of the hill." Really doesn't make me feel any better. Other than the fact I'm not going to jail for statutory rape. I was forty-six at the time. I had a daughter older than her. Meanwhile, little stripper girl came out of the bunk room, looking like you would think after a night rolling around and drinking, all on top of a night of dancing for dollars. I threw her an Egg McMuffin with cheese and told her she needed to go. We were leaving soon.

We saddled up and headed to Northeast Georgia for the funeral. I hate burying brothers. I hate to see their kids and parents at these funerals. But it is a part of how we chose to live. For most of us, it's not a matter of if, it is a matter of when.

We put Tripp in the ground and headed back to North Georgia clubhouse. I stopped at the food truck at the corner to get a beef burrito. When I pulled into the lot, I saw this civilian dressed in khakis pants and a button down handing out fliers. He was talking with Jack and had his back to me. Jack was facing me and gave me a look to go into the clubhouse. I went in and into the meeting room. Jack came in with this flier the guy was handing out and showed it to me, laughing, saying, "I told you she was eighteen," and handed it to me.

The flier had a school photo of the girl looking all proper and was asking for information on their daughter who ran away from home a few weeks before her eighteenth birthday. Now I really felt like ass and just packed up my shit and headed out for Savannah.

Had a great ride to Savannah and checked into a Haji hotel for the weekend and headed over to the clubhouse. I hung out with some brothers for a while then headed on over to Long County clubhouse to spend some time with Uncle Billy and CC. We took a ride, and then CC and I got into a local poker game he plays in. I took second place and won six hundred bucks.

Savannah national was epic as always. They are one of our strongest and largest chapters and really throw a great party. Ang and I ended up hooking up, and we had a great time together. We would go on to see each other whenever I traveled, and she was able to meet me where I was going.

We weren't dating exclusively. She lived nine hundred miles away, and I had gone through that with Heather, and I wasn't going to do that again. We both could do whatever we wanted as long as we didn't put it in the other's face.

Now, seeing the widow of a dead brother can make some brothers look at you the wrong way. I had one brother in particular give me a lot of shit about it, brother DJ. DJ and Voodoo were close, so I saw his take on it. But I wasn't treating her like a whore or disrespecting her. Everyone knew she was with me when we were both at an event and treated her accordingly. We would go on to see each other and had some really great times together till I started dating my now wife Jill in September 2014.

August 31, 2011. I headed to Long County to link up with CC so we could ride together to nationals in Phenix City. Phenix City is always a great time. Ang met me there, and we had taken a ride into Columbus for the day on Friday. That national meeting I was awarded my Knight's Cross. It is our second highest award in the club. Very humbling and proud moment for me. I broke one hundred thousand club miles on the ride home.

September 17, 2011. Our Rockland chapter somehow got us involved in the September 11 memorial run in New York City as road dogs. What a fiasco. There were about twenty of us and probably around two thousand plus bikes going on the run. It would start at ground zero and go on up the Henry Hudson over the George Washington Bridge to Palisades, New Jersey. After the run, we all headed over to a place called Cruckers for a barbecue. Our brother Chachie worked there, and he set it up.

Now, riding through Manhattan is one of my favorite things to do, so I was thinking, *Road-dogging this event is going to be way cool.* You know, get to rip up to the front or next intersection and basically ride without any rules or implications for your actions.

Well, it was a lot of frustration for sure. Blocking traffic on the Henry Hudson was no fun. There were more than a few "altercations." We had a brother rip off a license plate of a vehicle to remind the asshole driver we would find him (plate is still in our clubhouse). Little Billy and I teamed up, and we were blocking a cut through when a taxi with a Haji driver and oriental passengers pulled up behind us and beeped his horn. I got off the bike and approached the driver. I said, "Hey, buddy, it's going to be a while before you can go. All these bikes have to pass." We were spending about twenty minutes at each stop point. I walked back to the bike, and he laid on the horn again. Now I was pissed. I approached the car again and told him to stop hitting the horn and be patient. I turned to leave, and he did it again. Now I leaned down to the window, and I noticed the car was in park. I thought to myself, *Good. Don't have to worry about that.* I then said very nicely, "If you hit the horn again, I'm going to smack the shit out of you Haji, and for the record, if your relatives didn't attack New York City ten years ago, we wouldn't be here right now."

Well, he started yelling at me in Haji, and I just said, "Fuck it." I cracked him in the side of the head, and he fell over limp in the car. I pulled a twenty-dollar bill out of my pocket and threw it in the back seat at the Orientals who were freaking out at this point. I said I was sorry and "welcome to New York." Billy and I then split 'cause the taxi was blocking the road anyway.

Now Billy and I wanted to put distance between us and that intersection. We went into the open lane alongside the pack and opened it up. 111 miles per hour on the Henry Hudson! That's all Ms. Bettie has. She was rev limiting out. We rolled all the way to the front and then realized when we were on the George Washington Bridge, we were ahead of the lead escort still doing 111!

We got to the New Jersey side, and there were a ton of cop cars and cop bikes waiting for the pack. We braked hard and rolled up. Our bikes were smoking and brakes stunk. We just said, "They told us to let you know they will be here in ten minutes." We parked and got a couple of waters then headed over to Cruckers. That was an experience for sure.

November 10, 2011. Lil Billy, Jay, Johhny Law, and I headed out to North Georgia for their anniversary party. Then we headed out to Calhoun. I went to visit Heather's grave and see her family. I had lunch with her mom and son, Collin, at her mom's. I then went and spent the rest of the day and night over at Redneck's. Heather's mom let me have Collin for the night, and we did some fishing in Redneck's catfish pond, and I let him shoot a gun for the first time. He took a couple shots from my Walther PPK .380. The smile on his little face was priceless.

I remember this trip I took Redneck out in his wheelchair and took him over to his garage to start his bikes for him. He loved to listen to the bikes, and he would get all excited and start trying to mimic the sound. I wish I could've gotten to see him more, but there was a thousand miles between us.

I linked back up with my brothers for the ride home, and we set out at, like, 0300 hours. It's a little over nine hundred miles home.

We were on the eighty-five right outside of the northside of Atlanta. It was a real foggy, and we were fucking around, racing up the highway, reaching out, trying to turn each other's mirrors; and John was reaching out, looking back at, like, eighty miles per hour, trying to slap Jay when, out of nowhere, there were people aimlessly walking on the highway like a fucking zombie movie!

Johnny just missed some broad by inches! Fucking scary. We all braked hard, and then we saw the three-car wreck on the right two lanes. There were, like, four people just dazed and walking around on the road. We got passed the wreck, and we all looked at each other like, *What the fuck?* then throttled up and stopped fucking around after that. The rest of the trip was uneventful.

December 1, 2011. I brought Ms. Bettie into New Rock Harley-Davidson in New York; Billy was working there as a mechanic. I had scored the jug walls of both pistons, and the motor was knocking and shot. Probably on the September 11 run due to the abuse and the heat of the day. I had the extended warranty and decided to go with a remanufactured 96 cubic inch with the 103 cubic inch upgrade. Had to do it that way 'cause the insurance would only pay for the ninety-six-inch motor being that is what was in it. They ended up doing a new trans, primary, starter, and compression relief valves as well, all for fifty bucks!

This was the second motor under the warranty. This new motor would too be replaced down the road at around ninety-five thousand miles. That third one would be the charmer. Still in her, and now the motor has a little over 106 thousand on it and still running the road.

This concluded my most memorable rides for 2011. I ended the year with 24,202 club miles, and I visited out-of-state chapters twenty times.

CHAPTER 13

2012

January 11, 2012. I headed down to Fayetteville then onto Beaufort for nationals. This was an important one for my brother Wil. He and a bunch of guys were riding in from Corbin, Kentucky, to ask the nation for the opportunity to probate a chapter in Southeast Kentucky (SEKY). I got to meet brothers Curtis and Jodie that weekend, and it would be the beginning of awesome friendships and brotherhood. They would go on to patch out in January 2013. One of my favorite places to be.

February 1, 2012. Got another horrible phone call. A very young brother from our Long County chapter, Adam "Two Step" Huckstep, just home from Iraq, was killed by some asshole in a cage. He was only twenty-three years old and just made it home from one of the worst combat theaters in the Middle East. Fucking shame all because someone wants to save five seconds to answer a text while driving. People suck.

February 10, 2012. Lil Billy, Bermuda Mike, Mark "SK," and I rolled down to Long County for Two Step's memorial. It is never easy sending a brother off, but this was especially hard due to his age and not really getting the opportunity to get to know him better and watch him grow from a young man to an old graybeard. The time I did get to spend with him was priceless. He was a good kid and had a big heart and was always asking questions. He was a lady killer, always had a fresh one on his arm, and one in the batter's box, ready to step in. He also had a great straight right hand. Miss you, brother.

March 11, 2012. Well, the hits kept coming in 2012. Got the phone call that our brother Ian from now Calhoun County chapter had been killed in a wreck on his bike. Ian was originally from our Fayetteville chapter and was our national sergeant of arms for a really long time. He had since retired from contracting work and moved to a big, beautiful piece of property in Alabama. I got to spend a lot of time with Ian when Heather was alive due to me being in Alabama most of the time. Ian was as solid a man and brother as you will ever find. Love and respect, brother, till Valhalla.

March 23, 2012. Al, Kenny, and I headed down to Fayetteville for Ian's funeral. Most of the nation was there. Like I said, the hits kept coming. We received a phone call that our brother Luis Cordozo from our Beaufort chapter was involved in a wreck on his bike while en route to Ian's funeral and didn't survive his injuries.

Another life taken by some asshole in a cage. Luis loved his family, this club, his brothers, and most of all, this country. Luis was from Uruguay and came to this country with his family for a new life and found it here in America. We shared some awesome laughs, brother. Love ya.

March 29, 2012. Lee had sent me over to Southeast Kentucky probate chapter to check their progress and give him a report on them. At the time, the clubhouse was a probate member Frank's garage behind his house. I had learned that day they were in the process of getting a building leased, and we all rode over to check it out. We then went into town for some lunch. We headed back to the garage to have a few cold ones, shoot the shit, and play some pool. There was a pool table in the garage.

Well, some of the local "good ole boys" showed up, and it was a good time for a while. Then this one dude started talking some shit to a probate named Henry. I was waiting for Henry to smash him, but Henry was acting like his feet were stuck in concrete behind the bar. I finally walked up behind him (what a surprise, he was a lot taller than me). I looked at Henry, and he was way out of his comfort zone and had no idea no one talked to you that way, no one. I tapped ole boy on the shoulder, and he turned to me, still yelling at Henry. I hit him with my right elbow, and he folded to the floor. I looked at Henry and asked him why he didn't do that. He said they went back a long way, and this guy got this way when he had a few. I explained to Henry, "Your mother doesn't talk to you that way when you have your kutte on," and if he ever is nonresponsive again in this situation, it will be him folded on the floor.

A couple minutes later, good ole boy started to wake up and started running his mouth again. Frank stepped in and smacked him with a left and two rights, and it was night night for good ole boy again. I turned and looked at Henry and said, "That's the response that is expected at all times. Don't think. Act!"

Well, a few minutes later, good ole boy was coming around again, and this time he was a little bit smarter. He walked to the street to his bike before he started spouting off again, threatening to kill me and burn the garage down and all. We just waved and thanked him for his support.

About an hour or so later, he returned and parked his bike at the end of the driveway and was screaming and yelling that Henry owed him twenty bucks. As he was walking up the driveway, I was saying to myself, *This is rural Kentucky. He has to have a gun or just went home to get a gun. Either way, I believe he is armed.* So I decided to pull my gun out and aim on him and told him if he took one more step, it was double tap time. He stopped dead in his tracks and was screaming about twenty bucks still. I still couldn't believe Henry was letting this guy come up the driveway and realized Henry wasn't Wingmen material. I'd deal with him later. I asked Henry if he owed this guy twenty bucks, and he said he did. I told him to pay him so he could leave. Henry paid him, and he started down the driveway. He then stopped and turned again to threaten my life, saying he knew I was going to sleep in the garage tonight and he would come in the middle of the night to burn it down with me inside, etc. I had had enough of good ole boy and grabbed a pool cue and headed down the driveway. I'll give him credit; he came a-charging. I smacked him with the cue across the head, and he went down and out once again. I then proceeded to kick his legs apart and punt his nuts then stomped on both his hands with the heels of my boots.

This time, when he woke up, he immediately puked and went to grab his nuts and realized his hands weren't working too well. He made it to his bike and somehow was able to ride away.

It was at this moment I noticed the school bus with all the kids hanging out the window, watching this event. Then I heard, "Sir," from a little girl's voice. I turned to see Frank's eleven or twelve-year-old little daughter, Lucy, with her bright-red hair and big, wide blue eyes looking at me, holding what was left of the shattered pool cue. Yeah, they apparently saw the whole incident. She then proceeded to let me know that was her pool cue. I wanted to crawl in a hole. I apologized and told her I would replace her pool cue. That cue is on the clubhouse wall to this day. Oh, yeah, Henry didn't make it.

April 26, 2012. Headed to Calhoun for Ian's memorial. I stopped in Virginia to see my friend Kim. We rode the Blue Ridge Mountains and camped for a night in the woods. On my way to Calhoun, I was in a big highway truck stop, getting Wendy's, when a prospect from a club we had issues with was looking through the window at me while on his phone. I got my food and sat in a booth, facing the front windows. He is talking away and finally hung up and entered. I was sitting right on the edge of the booth, ready to play if need be. As he was walking, I was scanning for anything in his hands or visible weapons. He was tall, like six feet two or three inches tall, and his hands were huge, but he was skinny, maybe a buck sixty or seventy.

A little PSA: always check the size of a guy's hands. I don't care how strong you are or how hard you hit. If you got little girl hands, it isn't going to knock you out. Many great boxers didn't cut the mustard due to little hands and relied on points over knockout power.

He got a couple feet away, and I told him, "That's far enough." He stopped, extended his hand, and introduced himself to me. I didn't shake his hand but did let him know who I was. I then asked him if he was aware that our clubs weren't in good standing with each other at this time. The reaction on his face told me the answer was no. I then told him the only reason I wasn't smashing him was, there were a lot of people around who were just trying to eat lunch, as am I. I also told him, whoever he was talking to on the phone was either clueless to the situation as well or really doesn't like him too much, sending him in here to shake my hand.

Then I told him to turn around and walk out go to his bike and leave. He stood there for a moment and then realized I wasn't joking. I finished my meal and took a piss. Then I went out to my bike, and I saw prospect on the phone a few spaces down. I walked up and told him if he didn't leave now, I was going to beat his ass. He hung up and left.

July 27, 2012. I rode down to Fayetteville and linked up with Lee. We then headed out to Southeast Kentucky, where Chopper met us in Corbin. We had lunch with the chapter then went to their new clubhouse. I loved the building and property they leased. It was in the woods off a small tar and chipped road. There was a nice-size stream running through the area and an old bridge. We patched out Frank that night, and we all had a great time. The locals all came down, and again, I got to be around folks I would've never had a chance to meet if not for being a Wingmen.

August 17, 2012. I headed to Oak Grove for the annual pistol shoot. Once again, it was the devil's furnace all weekend with the heat and humidity. But this event I needed to go to. Our Devil's Elbow chapter was patching Johnny Demo, a.k.a. Johnny Loco, a.k.a. Good-Time Johnny. He and I had hit it off immediately when I met him as a prospect. We have been close ever since.

This weekend also saw a brother Joe Joe from our Opelika chapter, who had a prosthetic leg, break his good leg, leaving the ranch all banged up. Joe Joe once stayed at my house for a few days. I had an American Staffordshire named Lola, and she was a little crazy, and you never knew what she was going to do, like attack or lick you face. Well, Joe Joe was sitting on the couch, watching TV, and Lola just went at his leg. Fortunately for Joe Joe, she latched onto his prosthetic leg. The look on her face, wondering why he wasn't screaming in pain, was priceless.

August 25, 2012. This is the night I won the election for our national vice president's seat. I didn't aspire to be anything more than national sergeant at arms at the time. That was the best position ever.

"Butta, why did you smash that dude?"

"I don't know. Ask Lee. He gave me the nod."

Like I said, best position ever. I didn't have to really worry about anything, didn't have to really get involved with the "politics" end of anything. Only the security end, and I had all the local sergeant at arms to help me with that. It is the best job ever in a club in my eyes.

But myself and some other brothers had some issues with the way Chopper was handling himself in the vice president's position. I had talked to a few other brothers in the club with more time and experience than myself and asked if they would run. No takers, so I decided to run for the position, and I won.

This would bring Lee and I even closer and put us on a different level of working together. I was honored to be given the chance to step up by the nation. I dove in 100 percent and was ready for the challenge. I held the position for a total of four years, running unopposed the following three years.

August 30, 2012. Headed to North Georgia for nationals. This was my first national meeting as national vice president. Had a good meeting, and the club was very receptive to me being in the new position. I was looking forward to the challenge and getting more involved with the inner workings of the club.

September 29, 2012. Got the call that we had lost another brother, Sid, to another senseless wreck. Sid was a cornerstone to our Dawson County chapter. The news was devastating.

October 5, 2012. I headed out to our Dawson County chapter for Sid's funeral. Once again, having to see the devastation on his family and the club really sucks.

The Dawson County chapter had decided to start a scholarship fund in his honor for his daughter, Jayden. When she was finished with college, they kept the foundation going and give away scholarships in his honor every year to Wingmen's kids. My daughter, Melissa, was a recipient one year. Very awesome way to honor a brother and help brother's kids as well.

I don't have an actual date for this next story, but I know it happened right around the election for national vice president. It tells a big part of who I am and where I am from. Actually, most of the brothers from New York and New Jersey have a few of these to tell, and I know our Southern brothers get a kick out of them. It involves road rage.

I, as many, suffer from SRRS—severe road rage syndrome. I, for the life of me, can't keep my mouth shut when an asshole is driving in the left lane and should be at home on his/her couch instead. I can't count how many times I've gotten out of my vehicle and smashed some asshole at a red light or followed them home to beat their ass in their driveway in front of their family. Seriously, even my kids all have their favorite "Daddy road-rage incident." A big part of it was, I was really hitting the "gym gear" hard for the longest time back then (my cycle was the calendar year). I have since calmed down a lot and am finding my Zen.

Now, I'm not saying I was right, wrong, or politically correct in my actions, but it is a part of my life. I used to spend a lot of time on the phone with brothers when I would be driving, the old "kill two birds with one stone." I drive a lot for my job, and I have a pretty good commute each way to work, so why not get the calls out of the way while driving? Now, I am a law-abiding citizen and always use a Bluetooth, seriously always. Before Bluetooth, I would use the little earpiece thingy. My job relies on my license, and the fines in New Jersey are steep to say the least.

Well, one fine afternoon, I was driving home from work, and I was talking to my brother Weird Al from Oak Grove. We were bullshitting, and this asshat in an Audi cut in front of me then hit his brakes to continue on to the right lane. I held my rage and just got behind him, not missing a beat of the conversation with Al. This dude took an exit that I knew would be backed up at least twenty cars deep at the crossroad. I followed him off the exit even though mine was like five more away. The exit was really wide then tapered down to one lane. I waited till the right time, then I ran him on the left and basically pulled sideways in front of him. Now there were cars behind him, and he was trapped, and he was mine.

I exited my car and was walking toward my target, and I said to Al, "Hold on a second, brother." I now started laying into this asshole and let him know why I was standing at his car door, ready to rip his head off. Well, Al started yelling in my earbud at me to get back in my car (he had heard a few of these altercations before). I told him to shut up and then started smacking the idiot's face into his steering wheel. Al wouldn't let up, and I screamed, "Shut the fuck, Al." Well, this poor bastard started screaming, "Stop, stop. You got the wrong guy. I'm not Al. I swear I'm not Al!" All I could do was stop and start laughing uncontrollably. Dude was crying over and over, "I'm not Al." I got back in my car and drove home with Al giving me the riot act of how I would be shot if I did that down South.

I used to be so bad I had to change the vanity plates on my car that read TAT2ME 'cause I would get complaints called in all the time. Luckily, one of my uncles was a Bergen County judge. Seriously, though, if you want some good, free entertainment, call Joe Murray, Chaz, or myself while we are on our commute home. You will not be disappointed.

That pretty much wrapped up my riding for 2012. I ended the year with 19,861 miles and visited out-of-state chapters fifteen times.

CHAPTER 14

2013

December 4, 2012. Lee sent me to Southeast Kentucky again to observe the probates and give a report to the nation. I loved going there and spending time with brothers and riding around, checking out the area. Great place to go shopping for phew-phew toys as well. This trip was memorable 'cause I had tried to get some people to the clubhouse for a good time. I went online on some local meetup app to advertise the party. I ended up having this broad invite me to her trailer. Well, me being the club's public relations guy for the weekend there, I felt I'd have to oblige and all. I rolled over there with probate Jody, and when I got there, I told him if I didn't come to the front window and give the thumbs-up in a couple of minutes to bust in and kill everyone in the trailer.

Well, I went inside, and she was pretty hot, but her mother is hotter! I gave Jody the thumbs-up and proceeded to have a threesome with mother and daughter. I won't elaborate on the things we did, but they obviously have done this before and had a routine. It was a pretty wild time. Jody had reminded me that trailer walls were thin, and he and the neighbors pretty much heard the whole show.

January 21, 2013. I managed to talk Lee into giving the January national to Bergen County. Everyone was up in arms due to New Jersey actually having a winter, and they were worried about riding in the snow. I told the complainers, "Now the shoe is on your foot." I had ridden to every January national to date, except two.

Bergen knocked it out of the park as expected. Al had trays of food coming out fit for the finest restaurants every hour all weekend long. When you come to Bergen, you leave ten pounds heavier.

The weather cooperated as well. It was colder in Fayetteville than it was in New Jersey that weekend. I remember Darren getting hammered Saturday night, and I gave him my couch in the clubhouse. Then I ended up sleeping in the parking lot on the only couch left. I had watched a bunch of survival shows and thought I got this. One couch, one stripper flannel blanket, one sheet of plywood, and a burn barrel. What could possibly go wrong! I pieced together the burn barrel, the plywood, and the couch into a little hut and threw the little DNA-covered blanket on myself. *Not bad*, I thought. Well, I go lights out, and the next thing I know, I'm getting kicked and pushed and thrown off the couch by brother Yogi. Apparently, my blanket caught on fire, and Yogi was trying to put me out. The couch and my boots took the biggest hit. It was a fiasco for sure.

January 25, 2013. "SK" Mark and I headed to Southeast Kentucky again, this time to patch out Curtis and Jody. Lee met us there, and it was a great time had. Curtis and I have been thick as thieves ever since. He is one solid brother who is always there when you need him for sure.

March 14, 2013. I headed to Long County and stayed with Uncle Billy for a night, stayed in the Scooby-Doo bed! The next day, I hooked up with Rocket (not in a Rocket kinda way) to head to Northwest Florida chapter for their St. Patty's Day party. I remember Rocket and I on Route 10 west, doing, you guessed it, 111 miles per hour from gas stop to gas stop. It was a great ride, and the weather was perfect that time of year.

Northwest Florida put on a great show. They have tremendous local support. We all rode to Destin on Saturday and had lunch at the beach and just made our presence known.

April 18, 2013. I headed down to North Carolina and linked up with James. We then headed out to Southeast Kentucky. I told you I liked going there. We were going to just hang out with brothers and do some riding.

That Saturday morning, we took off on the bikes with no destination, just rode around and turned when we saw an interesting road. We ended up going down this road that then turned into a tar and chipped road. A few miles later, it turned into a gravel road. We saw an amazing house that was built at the bottom of a cliff. The cliff wall was in a semicircular shape and rose about one 150 feet to the top. The house was a large log cabin built right in the center of the clearing. There was a large pond in front of the house as well. It was a jealous maker for sure.

We continued on the gravel road for a few more miles, then it turned to dirt. We then noticed a bunch of beat-up mobile homes. We then noticed folks coming out of the mobile homes to see the bikes that you could obviously hear. They were all carrying guns and walking toward the road. We stopped, and I can see how this looked. Pretty sure this was a meth-making community. Upon further investigation, we could see a lot of fifty-five-gallon drums and garbage piled up everywhere. Now, they see two bikes in their front yards, and one of the riders is wearing a kutte; probably made them a little nervous. I just put my hand up and said, "Hey, man, we were just riding this rode, and this is where we ended up. We are going to turn around now and head back." I was totally expecting to be shot in the back.

We got back to the nice log cabin and stopped. James gave me a look like, "Holy shit, that was fucking close." I have to agree. I was surprised they let us just ride out of there without at least stopping us and asking us some questions.

May 6, 2013. Had to bring Bettie back to Empire Harley for another motor. She was burning oil bad and losing power. Ended up getting another remanufactured motor. Same 103 cubic inch set up. Third time would be the charmer though. That motor was put in with a little over 95,000 miles, and it is still in her and running strong, with a little over 206,000 miles on her. I did add Love Jugs mini cooling fans and a fan-assisted oil cooler. Started riding at night more (1) to help keep the engine cool, and (2) I'd rather take my chances with deer than all the morons texting and driving.

May 23, 2013. I didn't get Bettie back till the beginning of July. Jay let me use his Road Glide to go to Dawson County for nationals. I couldn't believe the cheap Jew didn't get cruise control on his bike to save a few hundred bucks! It is amazing how spoiled we have become with all the technology on bikes now.

June 4, 2013. Headed down to Fayetteville for Lee's thirtieth anniversary. Had a great time, and there were a ton of brothers there from around the country to show respect. As well as a bunch of local and out-of-state clubs who attended to show respect. Coming up on the big forty, brother. Your dedication to this lifestyle and this club is second to none! Por vida, boss. I broke one hundred thousand miles on Ms. Bettie on the ride home.

June 24, 2013. This is a trip that will show you the number of miles I can put in when I have to put in that work. Lee had sent me to our Devil's Elbow chapter area to handle a situation. I had asked Jack Baker and another brother from North Georgia, Johnny Drama, to meet me there for back up. I rolled into Devil's Elbow and handled business then had two Red Bulls and jumped back on my bike and headed home. I remember on the ride home, I was, I think, in Ohio, and I was so tired just looking straight ahead I heard this beep, and I looked to my left, and there was this cute girl hanging out the window of this little hooptie car with two other girls in it. She was flashing me her tits. I waved and said thank-you. She shouted to me, asking if I was all right. I yelled back yes, and she said, "Okay, 'cause I was hanging out the window for like two miles, and you didn't look!" That helped get the adrenalin going for a while. I ended up riding 2,241 miles in a little under thirty-six hours, with a meeting sandwiched in the middle.

August 31, 2013. Rockland County was hosting the Labor Day national, and I remember getting home Friday night to get some rest before returning in the morning for the meeting. I wasn't feeling good I had been running a slight fever. I had just gotten home, and I remember calling Wil and leaving a voice mail for him 'cause he hadn't yet arrived in New York by the time I'd left. I called him earlier in the day, and I knew he was heading a little north of Rockland first to visit a friend. He told me his ETA should be around 1900 hours. I had left at 2100 hours and hadn't heard from him.

I took a quick shower and racked out. About twenty minutes or so later, brother Rico from Oak Grove was calling my cell.

I answered, and he said, "Brother, there is no easy way to say this. Wil had a wreck and didn't survive."

I remember sitting up and saying, "Okay, is there anything we need to do now?"

He said, "No. I'm sorry. I know how close you two were," and that he loved me and prayed for me.

I was in such shock I just laid back down and went to sleep.

I woke up the next morning and told Lucille, and we cried, a lot. I sucked it up and headed up to Rockland County for the meeting. As you can guess, the mood of the party had changed for sure.

I really can't express enough about the man that our brother, Wil Williams, was. He was Wingmen though and though. He was a man's man. He was a war hero and a great family member who cared about his family and friends. I have a bunch of voice mails he had left me over the years. He would call me from Africa when he was contracting over there and have the local army guys leave me messages (hilarious shit). He would call and just let me know he was missing the club, his brothers, and his bike.

Back in the day, at an event in Orange County, Wil, myself, Fireman John, Stew, and Fat Mike were sitting at a table, having a beer, when Wil raised his beer and spoke. "We are some of the riddingest motherfuckers in this nation. It's not a matter of if but when." I remember cringing and taking the toast. Love you, brother, and miss the ever-loving shit out of you.

September 3, 2013. I went to Irvine, Kentucky, for Wil's funeral. I had a really hard time with this one. Wil and I were tight since I was a prospect, and I learned so much from him. Not just the club life but life in general. Wil was a deep human being and a really good soul. Now, don't get me wrong. He would cut your throat in a second for the right reason. He had women in every town, and they all knew it. He was a special person, and I'm honored he is my brother and that he respected and accepted me into his life.

His funeral was performed by the Masons. Wil was a Mason and had instructions in his will to have them do the honors. He was buried in his kutte as well. The ceremony they put on was nothing short of epic. Tremendous amount of respect and honor involved. I want to thank the Peacemakers Motorcycle Club in Kentucky for their part in the funeral as well. This was all taking place well away from our clubhouse in southern Kentucky and right in the middle of their AO. Wil had a great relationship (as does the Wingmen nation) with the Peacemakers MC. They had everyone meet at their clubhouse after the funeral. They fed us all, and we all had a great time reminiscing about Wil. Thank you again, Peacemakers MC. Much love and respect.

September 15, 2013. Al and I headed up to Rockland County to link up with the Rockland brothers to ride to Connecticut to attend the anniversary party for Charter Oak Motorcycle Club. Charter Oak is a 1 percent club that has had a great relationship with us for a few decades.

Well, Karate Joe and I were up in front, leading the pack. It was a beautiful day, and traffic was light. We were cruising in the left lane and just went over the Tappan Zee Bridge. Once on the other side, I took my helmet off and hung it off my mirror. Just as I did this, a state trooper pulled up alongside and lit us up.

I looked at Joe like, "What the fuck?"

He yelled to me, "Why did you take your helmet off?"

I replied, "We are in Connecticut."

He laughed and said, "No. Connecticut is about eight miles up the road!"

We pulled onto the shoulder to the left, and I got off my bike and walked back to the trooper's car. He was a massive Black man, I mean fucking huge.

When he was finished pulling himself out of the car he was wearing, I said, "Sir, I apologize, I was under the impression we were in Connecticut when we got over the bridge." I explained I was from New Jersey, riding with my New York brothers, and wasn't aware we were still in New York. He looked at me and asked for my license, registration, and insurance cards. I said, "Really? It's a seat-belt ticket, and I explained it was a misunderstanding."

Nonetheless, he wanted my credentials. I gave him them, and he noticed I had a gold PBA family card, which I was not giving him. He asked who gave me it, and I told him my brother-in-law is a retired Garfield, New Jersey, detective.

He responded, "You may want to call him."

Now I lost my shit. "You can go fuck yourself. Give me the ticket. I know that's all you got on me. I make twice the money you do. The fifty or so bucks won't hurt me," and so on.

He took my papers and got back in the car. About forty minutes later, he emerged again and handed me a thirty-five-dollar ticket and told me I should be more aware of my surroundings in the future. He got back in his car, and we were finally on our way again ticket in hand.

We finally made it to Charter Oak's clubhouse and had a great time. I remember they had boccie ball courts in their backyard. Chachi and I ruled the boccie courts all day, going undefeated.

September 15, 2013. Lil Billy and I headed to West Virginia chapter then onto Oak Grove for Wil's memorial. We were riding Route 64, about fifty miles outside of Lexington, when Bettie blew a front-wheel bearing. I was doing about eighty when it went, and it was a miracle I was able to keep her up. Billy was almost run over, trying to block traffic so I could get over to the right. The thing is, when a bike has antilock brakes and you lose a wheel bearing, you lose the brakes as well. Something to do with a magnet that runs something to the brake system that works off the bearing. So not only was I trying to avoid a death wobble, I had no brakes to boot. I was able to nurse her off an exit and into a gas station.

The girl who worked there was outside, having a cigarette. When I told Billy to check his phone for tow-truck services while I called my roadside service from my insurance, she butted in and said her boyfriend owned a tow truck and was on his way there. I hung up and figured, let's see what he has to offer.

I checked, and Lexington Harley-Davidson was forty-two miles away. Dude rolled up, and she walked over and told him I might need a tow. He walked over and asked if he could help. I figured, if he gave me a good price, I would pay it so as not to have to wait for the insurance company to find a service and have to wait around for them. I told him my destination, and he told me $400. I then knocked him out with a straight right hand. Ole girl screamed and went to run inside. Billy ran and got to the door first and told her if she called the cops, she would be next.

Boyfriend finally woke up and asked me why I hit him. I told him he made the mistake of insulting my intelligence by thinking he could charge me what he probably makes in two days for one trip. I had called my insurance while he was sleeping, and they told me they would have someone there in fifteen minutes. I told him not to make a big deal over what happened and to kiss his girl and be on his way, and he kissed her and left.

About a half hour later, the truck arrived, and Bettie was loaded up, and we were on our way to Lexington Harley. They were just getting ready to close. The service manager asked a tech to stay and fix my bike, and he did. I had a couple of pizzas delivered, and Billy got a couple of six-packs from a local gas station. Lexington Harley, hats off to you, and thank you for doing right by me and Billy. We got back on the road and made it to Oak Grove.

The next day, brothers from all over the nation came in to pay respects to Wil. The Oak Grove chapter planted a tree in the back-yard of the clubhouse with a plaque in Wil's honor.

September 29, 2013. I had been thinking of a way for Bergen to make some money and came up with the idea of a low country boil in the ghetto. Low country boils are a Southern thing, and my Southern brothers are always bragging on how good they are and how good they cook a seafood boil. I know Al can cook anything, and it will be just as, if not better than, the original.

The chapter agreed, and Al was confident, so the Bergen County, New Jersey, Low Country Boil in the Ghetto was born! We had a great turnout, and Al fucking killed it. RB had gotten these purple potatoes from Maryland, and it was a big hit. The tradition still happens every year in Bergen. If you haven't been, you should check it out. You won't be disappointed.

October 5, 2013. Myself and the Bergen brothers went over to the CC Riders MC clubhouse for their annual tattoo party. CC Riders are great guys, and we have supported each other's events since our chapter stood up. CC Riders has a few local tattoo artists come to their house and work on whoever wants to get poked. This event, however, would be the beginning of my tattooing career! CC Riders president is a guy by the name of Fatz. He is a great friend and one of the few guys outside of my club I like hanging out with.

Well, this night he and I had been hitting a bottle of Jack, and we decided to tattoo each other. It was nothing hard or difficult. Just a simple smiley face. Most of my body is covered in ink. I started young (fifteen). I have always put a great deal of thought into my ink, so this was a bucket-list item—get a meaningless tattoo while drunk. Fatz and I just took it one step further and decided to ink each other. Made for a great memory for sure. Love you, Fatz.

Well, I went on eBay a few days later and decided to get a tattoo gun. My goal was to ink my leg with some quotes I have lived by throughout my life. Well, I got this nice tattoo kit with two guns, tubes, needles, power supply, the whole nine yards. Problem was, I never used it. Then my brother Dustin Harts came to Bergen for a party, and we were admiring one of his new pieces of artwork, and I told him of my new toy. He immediately said, "Go get it and tattoo me!" Well, I did, and luckily, our brother Gator from West Virginia was there as well. He is an actual tattoo artist and owns a shop. He had to set up the gun for me and draw the design for Dustin. I can barely draw a stick figure. Dustin and I came up with a stick of butter. I went in and tried my best. This would start a domino effect of brothers wanting me to tattoo them. That is respect and love when a brother wants to get a tattoo from you that he knows is going to come out pretty awful! I have done a few sticks of Butta, a Butta baseball bat, and a few RFFDD tattoos since. Thank you, Fatz, for kick-starting my career! Love you, brother.

This would end my memorable rides for 2013. I rode and visited fifteen chapters for a total of 19,218 miles.

CHAPTER 15

2014

December 22, 2013. Adrian and I had gone to a local MC for a little get together. I met this broad. I'll call her Sadie. We were shooting the shit, and I told her we were heading over to another club's open house. I asked if her and her friend wanted to come with us. They did, but they caged it. It was December after all. We all met up and went inside. We said our hellos and settled in with a few drinks. Then a member of the hosting club came up to me with this guy who was from a club in Texas (he was visibly drunk). This guy shook my hand and introduced himself to me, and I returned the gesture then started talking with Sadie again. He noticed my Eagle, Globe, and Anchor and told me he was in the Navy.

I said, "Great. Good for you."

Then he patted me on the shoulder and said, "You gotta do a shot with me!"

I said, "Thank you, but I am drinking beer, and my friend is drinking vodka and tonic," if he wanted to buy us a drink.

He proceeded to slap me on the shoulder again and repeated, "You gotta do a shot with me!"

Now, if you know me, you know I fucking hate that. Grow the fuck up. What are you, sixteen? He went to say it again, and I cut him off.

I once again very politely said, "I am drinking beer, and my lady friend is drinking vodka and tonic if you really want to buy us drinks." He went to speak, and I said, "Okay, listen, we will do the shot. I drink whiskey. But after we do the shot, we are going to do what I want to do."

He got all excited and said, "Sure, I'll drink anything."

I then ask Sadie to back up a little bit. I fronted him and said, "I didn't say anything about drinking another shot. I said, we will do what I want to do."

Now he looked perplexed and was at a loss for words.

I said, "We will do a shot of whiskey, then we will go outside and fight."

He started to look around and then looked at me and said, "I don't want to fight you, man."

I said, "Good. Now you know how I feel because I don't want to do a shot with you." I told him it was nice meeting him and to run along now and enjoy his plane ride home. He just walked away.

Sadie looked at me and said, "Should I blow you right here or in my car?"

April 12, 2014. Lucille and I were pretty much done at this time, but she had asked me to take her to Phenix City for nationals. I didn't mind, and we headed out and got there Friday early afternoon. The national meeting ended on Saturday around 1200 hours, and around 1300 hours we got a call from Lucille's sister, Claire, our son, Dominic, had broken his arm and had real bad road rash from an accident on his moped. So we packed up and ran the roads back home to see to Dominic. I felt bad for her. She finally got out for a weekend, and it was cut short. Dominic healed just fine and was on two wheels again as soon as he could be.

April 25, 2014. Frankie the Elbow, Al, Adrian, Jay, and I had gotten a surprise visit from the one and only No-Hurry Murry! We were at the clubhouse and decided to take a ride to Lenora's. It is a local bar we frequented. Well, the joint was packed with a shitload of twenty-something-year-olds. We were all having a great time. Everyone left except for Murry and myself. Some Spanish dude was navigating his way through the sea of people and ended up directly in front of me. He was trying to push his way through and literally pushing some broad out of his way while she was waiting for the crowd to move forward herself.

I very nicely said, "Hey, chief, be patient."

To be honest with you, I don't even know what he said to me, but he was being loud and moving his head back and forth with each syllable. Next thing you know, he is slammed face-first into the digital jukebox on the wall next to me, and Murry followed through with all his weight behind him. Joe proceeded to toss him to the floor and then put the boots to him. Then just like that, Joe stopped and looked at me and said (in his very thick Queens, New York, accent), "No one is talking like that to you, Buttas."

I said, "Okay, Joe, thank you. Now let's just go outside."

He was ready to clean out the whole joint, I saw it in his eyes. Funny thing I noticed on the way out was, the digital jukebox was skipping on the same lyric over and over, and hence the name Jukebox Joe was born!

Now we had had a few drinks in us. We were in the parking lot, and I was calming the beast that resided in Murry (I'm really glad he is on our side) when a barmaid we know came out and said someone called the cops. We decided to stay in the parking lot since we both would blow dirty. Rather catch a disorderly or aggravated assault charge then a DUI. Well, we are waiting and waiting for like twenty minutes, still no po-po. Finally, Murry said, "Fuck it, I'm heading out." I jumped on my bike as well, and we left the parking lot. We were at a red light about a quarter of a mile up the road, and we see lights coming from our left, and here came two po-po cars screeching around the corner and went past us on our left. Murry blasted right, and I blasted left through the red light and beat feet home. Neither onc of us got pursued.

May 12, 2014. I headed to Fayetteville and hooked up with Lee and Super Dave. Dave was the club's national sergeant of arms at the time. We then rode to Maggie Valley, North Carolina, for a meeting with a local 1 percent club. We had some of our Nomad members there, and we were starting a chapter. Apparently, one of our guys and one of their guys grew up together and were still harboring some ill will. We met at a local bar, and Lee let me handle this meeting to see if I was learning and, I guess, to start assessing if I would make a worthy candidate to sit in his seat one day.

Their member and I had a great conversation, and we both ended with a mutual respect for each other and each club's concerns on the situation, and decided on an amicable solution. We went on to securing property, and our Western North Carolina chapter was started. If you want to ride roads that use all sides of your tires, that is the place to go.

May 24, 2014. Bergen hosted nationals. It was the chapter's ten-year anniversary. Once again, Bergen hit it out of the park. Al worked his magic and cooked to feed our brothers like the Viking warriors they were. We had tremendous civilian support as always, and the weekend went off without a hitch.

We rent the meeting hall at the Hilton Hasbrouck Heights for the meeting. It is at the top of the building, I believe around twenty-five or so stories high. I love seeing the looks on new brothers' faces who have never been to New Jersey or New York when they see the Manhattan skyline for the first time.

June 10, 2014. A very good friend of mine by the name of Ox ran the roads with me to our Southeast Kentucky chapter. Ox was interested in the club and was starting to hang around. We rode through some pretty crazy thunderstorms on the way, I remember.

Once there, we had a great time as usual in Kentucky. The local toothless hooker with $5,000 tits was there (she lived in the trailer park down the road; God, I love this chapter!) along with the regular locals as well as a bunch of brothers. I had Ang meet me there as well.

The chapter was patching out a brother named Possum. Well after he patched out, he proceeded to get very drunk very fast. He decided to get very disrespectful and belligerent with me, though he thought he was just being funny. I remember pinning him to a wall and telling him he would regret this in the morning when he was sober and would then understand why I would be beating his ass.

Next morning, I headed back to the clubhouse and find Possum. He was apologizing like a hooker in church. Apparently, someone had reminded him of his fate. We went into the meeting room, and I laid an elbow and a left hand on him. He folded to the floor. Well, he started leaking badly from his right ear. We woke him up, and he ended up going to the hospital to get his ear stitched back on; it was kind of hanging off. Welcome to the club. He and I would go on to be close brothers. Then he ended up a quitter some years later. He is one of the ones that it hurt when he left, and I couldn't understand why he would walk away. But he is gone, and it is what it is.

Ox had a great time, and we rode home without incident and had great weather for the ride home. Ox started some good relationships with some brothers.

August 27, 2014. Our brother Chopper had had a wreck a few weeks before and was banged up badly in the hospital. It is a miracle he was even alive. He was T-boned at an intersection by a tractor trailer that ran a red light. He was on one of his many Dynas. The bike was flat. I shit you not, it was as flat as you can make a Dyna on its side.

I went to Phenix City to see him in the hospital. He was in good spirits and had me wondering if he was immortal. Don't get me wrong, he had some serious injuries and had a long road to recovery, but I couldn't imagine anyone surviving that type of hit. I thank God he did. Love you, Chop.

From Phenix City, I rolled up to Calhoun County and hooked up with my brothers Ghangis and Chief and headed to Oak Grove for nationals. Had a great time in the beautiful Kentucky furnace heat! Hey, Sapper, you forgot something in the port-a-john!

September 24, 2014. I headed to Phenix City again to hang out with Chopper in his rehab facility. He was definitely himself again and driving the staff crazy. I then headed to Calhoun County to visit Heather's grave and meet with her daughter, Ms. Alexis, for lunch. From there I ran up to Dawson County for Sid's annual memorial run. It was another great long weekend visiting and hanging out with brothers and their families.

October 25, 2014. I headed to Cherokee, North Carolina, where a bunch of us from multiple chapters had met up to ride the Dragon's Tail. For those that don't know of the Dragon's Tail, it is an eleven-mile stretch of road with 318 curves. It is awesome, and every year riders from around the world go there to test their skills. Our prospect from Dawson County, Cory, would later go on to become a patch holder and lead the way for our Maggie Valley Western, North Carolina, chapter. Cory's uncle owned a hotel in Cherokee, and we all got rooms. We went old-school party Friday night in the parking lot. I remember the Southeast Kentucky probates all being there.

We woke up to fifteen degrees and frost on our bikes Saturday morning. We all had a great breakfast and then headed out to the tail.

I had set up a go pro on Ms. Bettie's tour pack and have some great footage from that run. I remember my brother Skid and I just tearing shit up! At one point, we came in hot on some *rub* on a Road Glide, and we gave him about half a mile to move over and let us pass. Well, he didn't, and I finally cut under him in a left curve, and Skid followed. When watching the video, you see me hit the curve with Skid in tow then the guy wobbling and moving to the side of the rode and flipping us off.

This would end my most memorable runs for the year of 2014. I visited fourteen out-of-state clubhouses and ended the year with 20,430 miles.

CHAPTER 16

2015

January 14, 2015. I headed to Fayetteville and then hit our Effingham clubhouse for a night. I then went to Long County for the patching of our brother, Bama. Bama is a young stud who has grown into a great man over the years. I spent a lot of time with him as a prospect and wanted to be there for his big day. He has since transferred to our Savannah chapter and has been a great addition to that chapter. Bama is my personal bulldozer when I need shit wrecked. He carries those lunch boxes around for when the time is right. Love you, brother.

I once again rode the roads to Northwest Florida with Rocket for nationals. Once again, everyone got the Crestview crude, and some brothers were sick for weeks. I think it's all the trailer-park hookers in the area.

February 7, 2015. I had started dating my now wife, Jill, September 26, 2014. Lucille and I had tried and tried, but as the Gordon Lightfoot song, "If You Could Read My Mind" goes, "The feeling is gone, and I just can't get it back." Jill and I had a history. We had dated in high school. Then I went into the Marine Corps, and her family moved back to Vermont. Back then there weren't cell phones, emails, or even answering machines, I think. So we just lost touch. Then lo and behold, *Facebook*! We had found each other on there and started talking in late 2013. We were both in the same predicament, a marriage that had failed, but for some reason, we both hadn't left yet.

Well, we finally decided to give it a go and see what happens. I told Lu, and Jill told her husband. It wasn't an easy decision or road to hoe, but I thank God we did. I don't know where I'd be today if not for her in my life. She has been my best friend, and I love her with all my heart and want to grow "older" with her.

So on this date, Jill attended her first Wingmen event. We drove up to Rockland for their winter freeze party. She got to meet all the local brothers, got some sideways glances from some of the ole ladies, and six years later, we are in our second year of marriage, with four new kids, an English white Lab, a fat cat, a golden retriever with OCD, and a pitch-black Beagle Lab mix! I love you, babe. XOXO forever.

April 11, 2015. Jill's first ride with me on Ms. Bettie was to Keansburg, New Jersey. It was like thirty-six degrees outside. I told her to dress for the weather, not for vanity. Well, she didn't listen and froze her ass off. Though she never complained. We went to a bar/restaurant there called the Stadium. I used to go there with Big Bobby all the time. We had a good time watching the local drunks get hammered and sing songs like people wanted to hear them sing.

Once, some years back in, like, 2001 or 2002, I broke a urinal with a guy's face in the men's room there. Big Bobby and I had been there all day, drinking and eating steamers when four guys were walking down the street and stopped to look at our bikes. I said to Bobby, "One of these morons is going to do something stupid." Just then, one of them throws a leg over my bike for a picture. I got over to them and smashed the one with the camera, and the other two ran. Dude on my bike jumped off and ran into the bar like an idiot. I chased him into the men's room, where I proceeded to kick the shit out of him. I smashed his face into the urinal while he was on all fours, and it just shattered. We didn't go back there for a while.

We ended up hearing they were illegals and were all arrested that day. Back then they used to actually arrest illegals. Imagine that. So we started going to our joint again. In 2019 Jill and I took a ride there, and it was knocked down, and they were building condos on it. I remember just sitting in the middle of the road, blocking traffic for a couple minutes, with my mouth wide open. I have some of my fondest memories of Big Bobby from that place.

Let me tell you all about my friend, Big Bobby. Bobby and I met in 1990 through a mutual friend. We had become close friends, and Bobby was a regular at my house and considered family by Lucille and the kids.

Well, Bobby had had a lot of physical issues due to his size. He had bad knees, hips, and back. He had a few not-so-minor but not life-threatening wrecks on his bike recently and was out of work as well due to his condition. Bobby was an old-school biker to the fucking core! He had crack whores running the streets for him and slung some weed to get by. But Bobby had some demons he was fighting as well and tried to take his own life. I was supposed to go camping with three of my kids one weekend. Lucille was in Arizona, visiting family with Melissa, who was an infant at the time. We ended up getting a horrible storm, and we canceled the camping trip. Bobby had been really depressed Lately, and I called to check on him. After a few hours and no answers to my calls, I decided to go to his trailer and check on him. I get there, and he was flat on his back, foaming from the mouth. I called 911, and it took six of us to get him into the ambulance. He was out for a few days, and while he was out, the doctor had told me he had enough cocaine in his system to kill a couple of horses.

On the third day of him being in the hospital, he woke up. I was there, and when he was able to talk, he asked me who found him. I told him I did and that if I would've known he was going to off himself, I would've liked a goodbye at least. He told me to fuck myself. Bobby had mixed one half ounce of cocaine in a glass of water, drank it, and lived to tell about it.

Bobby had gotten out of the hospital and was pissed at me that I called 911 and he lived. I didn't know how to take that and told him we could've talked about what he was planning and, like I said, at least have a nice goodbye. I know that sounds horrible, but no one knows what another person is going through truly. If he was at the point of not being able to take it anymore, then so be it; it is his life.

I knew Bobby well enough to know he would never do that unless he truly felt it was his best or only option. Bobby was in a tremendous amount of physical pain all the time. He was always the one riding and partying and fucking crack whores. His life changed dramatically and was not only polar opposite but, like I said, filled with physical pain as well. Bobby wasn't one that was going to depend on others to take care of him.

We were barely in touch with each other for about a year or so when I got the news he had passed away from a mutual friend. His family (he two had brothers) didn't notify anyone and just had him cremated with no service whatsoever. It was a very sad, hard day in my life for sure. Bobby was larger than life, and when he walked in the room, he fucking owned it. Love and miss you, Big Bobby.

April 17, 2015. This was Jill's first long ride on a bike. We headed to Jacksonville, North Carolina, to hang out with the deadhouse crew. J-Ville was a relatively new chapter and was made up of a bunch of young Marines from Camp Lejeune. They had a young, reckless, off-the-chain, gonna-change-the-world mindset. Jill and I had a great time on the ride down, and she did awesome. Never complained dealt with my three-and-a-half-minute gas stops, the whole nine. She logged her first of many over one-thousand-mile weekends. We rode 1,315 miles. She would soon find out this was considered a short to medium trip!

May 10, 2015. Got a phone call that we lost a brother from J-Ville by the name of Dennis Anderson. He was a young, full-of-life brother who as many fought for this country and saw the worst humanity has to offer and then was taken to soon on a motorcycle. Dennis was the life of a party and a great brother and Wingmen. Miss you, brother RFFDD.

May 15, 2015. Jay and myself headed down to J-Ville for Dennis's funeral. We left a day early and decided to take the Turnpike to 13 to 17. The long way going over the Chesapeake Bay Bridge. Well, we were on the tail end of the bridge doing around eighty-five miles per hour when I blew my back tire. I was riding right of Jay. Well, Ms. Bettie hung a left right into the side of Jay. Then her and I proceeded to bounce off the big man, and we were heading right for the guardrail and the side of the bridge. All I could think of was, *Man, I hope there is a boat close by.* I got off the throttle and pulled Bettie to the left by leaning as far as I could and finally straightened her out. We made it off the bridge and into a gas-station parking lot.

Whatever I ran over left a perfect half-inch hole right in the center of my tire. Now it was, like, 1730 hrs. I knew there was no way we were plugging the tire, so I got on the phone and called Virginia Beach Harley-Davidson. I got their service department and told them of my situation. Mind you, they close at 1800 hrs. I explained I was going to Jacksonville for a brother's funeral scheduled for 1300 hours the following day. They put me on hold and then got back on the line to tell me there was nothing they could do for me tonight. Now, I was trying not to blow a gasket 'cause I needed them to fix my shit. After some going back and forth, they told me they would pick up the bike at 0700 hours in the morning, and it would be the first thing they would work on in the morning. At this point, I knew it was useless to argue any further. I got a room and told Jay to head on to J-Ville without me. I would be there as soon as I could tomorrow.

The flatbed showed up around 0645 hours, and we headed over to the dealership. They got Ms. Bettie up and running and after signing the paperwork and paying the $50 deductible for the tire and work I laid into the service manager and gave him a full dose of Joey. I have broken down in a lot of states, and never have I been turned away as long as someone answered the phone at a dealer. *Never.* I let him know if I miss my brother's service, I would be back to further discuss the events.

I ended up back on the road at 0915 hours. According to the GPS, I have to make up forty-five minutes to be on time. Well, I hit 13/17 south and opened her up and had no regard for myself or anyone else. I was flying running lights, passing on the right and the left. I was using every ounce of my riding skills to get there on time. Well, it was, of course, inevitable that I pass a local sheriff with Bettie's throttle wide open. I blew past him and figured if he came out and caught me, I would stop; if not, I wasn't letting off the throttle.

Now, I didn't see him pull out, so I thought, wow, maybe he was asleep or getting a blow job or something. Then I saw them way in the distance in my mirrors. The familiar lights of the law. Now, mind you, I was literally an hour or so out and did make up the time I needed to as to not be late. I decided to pull over and wait for him. I knew he was coming for me. I got off Bettie and took my helmet off, and when he rolled up and got out of his car, I didn't know what came over me, but I just lost it. I basically charged up on him and laid into him with all my frustration from the trip's events so far. I just started screaming, "I got a fucking blowout, almost died on the bridge. Fuck Virginia Beach Harley-Davidson. I'm going to bury a brother, and I can't fucking be late." Yada yada. I don't know how he didn't shoot me. I was so erratic. He stayed unbelievably calm and waited for me to get winded and stop my rant. Then he asked me if I knew how fast I was traveling on a 50-mph road. I replied, "Yes, 111 miles per hour, that is all she has." I just looked at him. I was pretty defeated at this point, and he could sense my disappointment. He asked if I was attending the funeral for SSGT Dennis Anderson. Apparently, he had known of Dennis's accident or might have known Dennis from the Marines, I didn't know. I said yes. He offered his condolences for my loss and asked me to please slow down. He looked at his watch and let me know I would be on time, barring any accidents.

I have to admit, I was blown away. I thought for sure I was leaving in cuffs. I thanked him and shook his hand, jumped on Bettie, and threw her into gear. I literally pulled into the parking lot of the funeral home just as they were opening the front doors. I pulled into the parking lot, and my phone said it was 1258 hours. I got to pay my brother the respect he deserved and earned. Love you, Dennis.

May 26, 2015. Got a call that my brother Jeff Davis had lost his wife, Donna. On May 29, 2015, Daniel from our Rockland chapter and myself set out to West Virginia chapter to pay our respects to and support our brother. Now, Daniel was never the sharpest tool in the shed. I used to call him Magilla, as in Magilla the gorilla. He was as big as a wall and just about as much common sense. We left from my home at around 1300 hours. We had gotten to Carlisle when it started to rain and the temperature began to drop. I started to put on my rain gear and asked Danny what he was waiting for. He replied he didn't pack his rain gear. Luckily for him, I had Jill's gear in the bags. He needed gloves, hoodie, rain gear, the whole nine yards. I asked him why he didn't pack anything for rain or lower temps. He replied, "It was nice when I left my house!" I didn't even know how to respond 'cause he was serious.

We got to Pax in the middle of the night and racked out at the clubhouse. The next morning, brothers, family, and friends started showing up at the clubhouse. The church was about sixty or so miles away and up and down mountains and back roads. Brother Jeff had Donna's ashes on his bike, and this ride was for her. My brother Gator and I were up front with me front right. Jeff and Fireman John were behind us, and then the rest of the Wingmen pack followed by civilians.

Now, Gator and I have beaten a lot of roads in West Virginia together. Whenever we are there together, we go for a ride and tear it up. So we were about twenty or so miles from our destination, and we were starting to dip a little more into the corners and come out of them a little stronger. Finally, I looked over at him and asked if Jeff and Fireman knew where they were going. He smiled and said, "Yes, they do," then down shifted and took off. I was right next to him, and we tore that shit up for the remainder of the trip. We had gotten to the church and parked, took off our helmets, and just smiled, knowing we just beat that road up and that Fireman was probably gonna be pissed!

About twenty or so minutes later, the pack rolled in, and Fireman beelined right for us! "What the fuck, Butta? You can't control your urges even for a funeral?" Gator slipped out somewhere and left me to the ass-chewing. Then brother Jeff came up and gave me a big hug and had tears in his eyes and said, "Donna wouldn't have had it any other way. She loved it!"

After the service, we all headed back to the clubhouse and did our thing. Jeff and I had a nice talk, and I admired his strength. They had been together since they were young, had kids and grandkids. Tight, tight family. I hate to see my brothers in pain. Love you, brother, and we need to get together more often, brother.

July 3, 2015. Jill and I head to West Virginia for their annual Fourth of July party. I love Pax. They are a little town who comes together for certain holidays, and you really feel like you are living in America the way it was meant to be.

The local park is used, and everyone cooks and sets up tables, and there are kids running around. Just good family stuff. Our brother Dave Strick sets up the fireworks display every year. He spends months getting it rigged up for the big day.

Brothers arrived from all over the nation. Gator and I took a bunch out to the gorge for some great riding and sightseeing. Just a really good event.

On the way home, the weather was perfect. The roads weren't crowded. Great tunes on the radio, and we were just lost in the ride. That was when Jill tapped my shoulder and pointed to the fuel gauge. I was on E, I mean E, and the digital thingamajig that tells you how many miles to empty was already on LO. We were on a stretch of 76 east in the mountains, and there was nothing. Every exit was desolate. Finally, I pulled off an exit that said there was an Exxon station. We went a mile down the road off the exit, and it was there! Only problem was, it was abandoned! Now I was telling her to watch the mile markers, thinking we would be calling triple A soon. We rolled at least another seven or so miles and finally came to a small town with a gas station. I put 6.3 gallons of gas in a six-gallon tank, with a picture of the pump display to prove it.

July 25, 2015. The Saturday morning of our chopper show, I took about ten or so out-of-state brothers to my job for a tour of the plant. I got permission from the director, and security was alerted of our coming. I wanted to show my brothers where I spent most of my life. They hear about the plant all the time. Most of the time when I am on the phone with them, I am at work, so I thought it would be cool to show them the plant and go over what we do there.

We went from building to building, and I explained the process of the treatment. They were truly interested, and it made for a really good time. Afterward I gave a pop quiz, and Uncle Billy got an A+!

I then took them to a place in Newark that we eat at a lot while working overtime mostly on Saturdays. It is called Krug's. The best cheeseburgers in New Jersey and the best calamari. Go figure, it is run by drunken Irishmen, and they have the best calamari.

We all ended the day at the clubhouse for the chopper show, and everyone thankfully got home safe after another successful chopper show put on by Bergen.

November 11, 2015. Headed to Long County, where I stayed at Uncle Billy's in the Scooby-Doo bunk bed. Then he, CC, PD, and myself headed to Cherokee County for a party there. Always good to be in CHECO and see my brothers Carney Carl and Stogy the Jew. From there the four of us, along with Stew, Angel, and Kyle from Devil's Elbow chapter, headed over to the North Georgia chapter for their anniversary party.

This concluded my last ride for the year 2015. I ended the year with nineteen thousand miles and visited out-of-state chapters seventeen times.

CHAPTER 17

2016

January 10, 2016. Headed down to Florida to visit my grandson then head over to Tampa then onto Crestveiw for nationals. On the way, I stopped by to see my friend Kelli's daughter, Ashley. She had recently married and had a baby. So I stopped in Daytona and got to see Miss Smasher and little baby Jordan. Thank God for social media and being able to keep in touch with certain people. I love Miss Smasher and consider her family. She is one of the kindest and thoughtful people I know. She is an awesome mother and recently had a set of twins as a surrogate mother for a friend of hers and her husband Kenny.

Miss Smasher, it is an honor to have watched you grow into a beautiful, caring, and kind woman. I know your mom is so proud of you. I love you, Miss Smasher.

So from Daytona I headed south to Delray Beach to visit my daughter and my little prince. On the way, I noticed my gauges were going in and out and having issues with the radio and cruise control. After getting to my daughter's, I called West Palm Beach Harley and brought Bettie over to them. Ended up being a couple frayed wires in the wiring harness going up into the neck.

I spent a couple days in Delray with my grandson and got to go for our first walk together. The last time I saw him, he was still crawling. I hate that my grandkids (since this event, my daughter has had a beautiful daughter named Cecilia) live in Florida and I live in

New Jersey, but it is what it is. What really sucks is, I hate Florida. Nothing about that state is attractive to me whatsoever.

I then rode up to Tampa to our Central Florida chapter to hang out with brothers Rhino and Simon. Bama had ridden down from Savannah to hang as well. We hit Ybor City for a local bike night that night, and of course, it fucking poured.

We headed out in the morning to Crestview, our Northwest Florida chapter, for nationals, and yes, still pouring. It was bad, and brother Rhino didn't have rain gear, so we stopped at a fast-food joint to eat and see if the weather breaks. Some dude started talking to Rhino, and he wasn't the most personable of persons and basically told the guy to fuck off. The guy had some nuts and started to go back at Rhino verbally till Rhino stood up. We got back on the road 'cause the rain wasn't letting up and hit a Harley dealer outside of Jacksonville, I think, and Rhino dropped, like, $600 on new rain gear, gloves, and a full-face helmet. Yep, you guessed it—sunshine the rest of the way!

In Crestview Bama got into it with a few gangbangers and handed them the lunch boxes for their disrespect. He ended up in a cell for a while till everything was sorted out. Just another day, Bama, just another day!

February 18, 2016. Truly a very sad day. I was at the gym when I got a chapter text saying brother Jay had passed away from a heart attack. I remember I was in a stairwell and literally couldn't breathe. I thought it was a joke, and I called Little Kenny, and he assured me it wasn't. Our brother was dead.

Jay had been found on his couch by his girlfriend a few hours before. He was gone, and there was nothing paramedics could have done for him. You just never know when you won't wake up, brothers. We as a chapter were devastated. Jay was larger than life and just coming into his own as a patch holder and leader in our chapter.

Jay and I rode many miles to many clubhouses and events side by side. He was a great road dog and never complained to my style of riding like you rented it from point A to point B. Jay was a great brother and Wingmen. He truly loved this club and his brothers.

Best off, Jay was pretty much "drama" free, which is hard to find these days.

Jay was Jewish, and his family, following Hebrew tradition, had twenty-four hours to get him in the ground. The chapter was all there, with a lot of out-of-state brothers who were able to make the trip on such a short time frame. We buried our brother and then celebrated his life together as his brothers. Love and miss you, Jay Man.

March 19, 2016. Myself, Danny "Magilla Gorilla," and Chaz rolled down to Slaughter Pen, Virginia, chapter. On the way down, Bettie blew an oxygen sensor. I made it there, but she wasn't making it home without a replacement. Couldn't find a dealer or shop with one available and ended up U-hauling her home. Slaughter Pen is definitely Bettie's kryptonite. I broke down with her way too many times either on the way there or on the way home.

Anyway, on the way, we took the long way down 81 south to 66 to 17 as to avoid tolls and traffic. We hit some weather. It started snowing, and Danny and Chaz were not equipped for the cold, wet stuff. They ended up tapping out about seventy miles out of Slaughter Pen and got a hotel room. I charged on and attended the party in their honor!

April 15, 2016. Myself, Igor, Little Kenny, Mike D, and Al rolled down the 95 to attend Slaughter Pen's anniversary party. We all had a great time. Brother Corey rolled in with a huge dead pig and worked his magic on the grill. On the ride home, Igor and I decided to roll the back roads back home 17 to 66, 81 then 78, home. Well, bad move. We hit a spot on 78 east, where we were stopped dead for a few hours due to a new bridge being constructed, and they were moving some pieces with a crane and shut down the road. Still had great weather at least!

April 29, 2016. Myself and Keith rolled down to North Georgia for the memorial of brothers Clink and Mudcat. Both brothers passed a few weeks earlier and just three days apart from cancer. Clink was a longtime Wingmen married to Ms. Gina, who is one of the greatest ole ladies you'll ever find. Brother Mudcat was a lot younger and was a good, solid brother who was as country as country can get.

Clink and I would spend a lot of time on the phone when I wasn't down South and able to see him. He battled a lot of health issues, and it limited his travel. Brother Mudcat, as to my recollection, was fine then was diagnosed with a very aggressive cancer that took him very quickly.

It fucking sucks, brothers. You never know what tomorrow brings. Be yourself and do what you want to do each and every day. Let the ones you love know you love them and the ones you hate know you hate them. Tomorrow may not come to do so.

May 20, 2016. Sent my official letter of intent to run for national president. Lee and I had spoken throughout the year, and he informed me he would not run again and would endorse me for the position. A longtime patch-holder brother, David Tope, had already put in his letter of intent back in January. He and I spoke, and I informed him I would wait to do so two weeks prior to the national meeting scheduled in Savannah.

David and I were on the same page with a lot of issues and mindset. But polar opposite on others. It was a long year to say the least to get to the election night. It was a lot of drama and defending my name and ways.

May 26, 2016. Jill and I headed to Fayetteville as a stopover before heading on to Savannah for nationals. We spent the night at the clubhouse with brothers and ole ladies then hooked up with RB and his ole lady, Mar, to ride together to Savannah.

The meeting and all subsequent events were as always in Savannah above the bar. The weather for the party Friday and Saturday actually was awesome. It was one of the first times being in Savannah and not sweating balls all the time.

However, the ride home was a little bit different. Tropical storm, Bonnie, hit hard Sunday morning. I remember everyone else saying "fuck it" and sleeping in. Well, Jill and I suited up and hit the 95 north. It was crazy rain with some pretty serious winds. We got to mid-South Carolina, and boom, dead stopped. I ran the shoulder for about three or four miles and then came upon two state troopers stopped and blocking the highway. One rolled his window down and informed me that the road ahead was closed until further notice.

Now the toes of my boots got water running over them. I was not about to just sit there in the rain. The trooper could read my mind and yelled, "Don't even think—" That was all I heard as I dropped the clutch and went past them on the right. I knew they weren't going to chase me, and worst-case scenario, they radio ahead and try to block me in at the next roadblock. Well, neither happened, and we rolled right up 95 with absolutely no one else on the road.

We were just north of Baltimore now, and we were both drenched straight through. I don't skimp on gear, especially rain gear. But no matter how fancy, good, or expensive the gear, sooner or later, water will find its way in. I remember asking Jill if she wanted to stop and we would get a room. She just said, "No. I'm okay if you are okay." Fucking trooper she is, I tell ya. I really wanted to tap but wanted her to be the one I could blame it on. She never tapped, and we were home in around fifteen hours. I knew then she was the one.

My wife has ridden all over with me, and I only do straight-through trips to the likes of Devil's Elbow, Phenix City, and Calhoun County. Those are all one-thousand-mile to eleven-hundred-and-change one way trips done in between thirteen and sixteen hours.

July 15, 2016. Jill and I headed to Southeast Kentucky for some R and R. We hung out at the clubhouse Friday night and had a few adult beverages and played no-limit hold 'em poker before turning in for the night. Brothers Gabe, Cheyenne, and Johhny "Pain" were there.

Saturday morning, we all went to breakfast then for a ride to Cumberland Falls State Park. Had a great day just riding with brothers and seeing what the beautiful state of Kentucky has to offer.

Jill and I went and hit a few flea markets as well. I love "shopping" the flea markets there. It is amazing the things you can find. I once bought socks, bear jerky, ammo, and a gun from the same guy!

August 5, 2016. I rode to Dawson County and North Georgia to do some politicking for my election. I hated that part. At the time, I had been a patch holder for almost ten years, and in a national position for most of them. I figured, if you didn't know me or what I was about by then, well, you probably haven't been paying attention. But

I used it for an excuse, I guess, to get on my bike and ride. So off on the campaign trail I went.

August 19, 2016. I rode to Effingham County, Georgia, for more politician games and also headed to Long County for an emergency national executive council meeting that had been called. It was decided on Long County's location 'cause they had just had a new clubhouse built. The old one burned down, and they were just about ready to have the new one finished, so we figured, good spot to hold the meeting and fill their new house for the first of many times to come.

August 26, 2016. The Wingmen nation had decided by a vote to elect me their new national president. It was a humbling and exciting feeling. I was ready for the next step and was glad the politicking was finally over (or so I thought) and I could jump into the deep end of the pool once again and either sink or swim.

September 2, 2016. Jill and I rode to J-Ville for nationals. My thirtieth consecutive one and my first as national president. Damian from our Savannah chapter was voted in as national vice president. I had appointed "DDD," Triple D Doug, from Savannah as our new national secretary. RB from Bergen County would be national treasurer. Stew would become my national sergeant at arms. Tom "my real name ain't Smith" was in our Little River, North Carolina, chapter. He would soon transfer to Huntsville, Alabama, where we would assist in standing up a probate chapter. He and Flo from Northwest Florida chapter would be assigned as regional sergeant at arms under Stew's command. This was the group of guys I chose to help bring the nation to a different light while never compromising our earned respect, history, and most of all, tradition.

I had asked for and received the chance to lead the Wingmen nation, and I was given the chance along with the huge responsibility that goes with it. I received my Order of the Eagle award at this meeting for all my accomplishments in the club to date. It is our club's highest honor and was a very humbling moment for me.

November 10, 2016. I headed to North Georgia for their anniversary party. I went to hang out with my brother Bob from Dawson County first. He and his wife, Karen, had just had a little baby girl named Zoey. I hung out with them for the day, and they fed me breakfast and lunch. Bob is a very special brother to me. He and I have a great relationship for just about the whole time I have been in the club. He came in and patched right after me with our Dawson chapter as a probate member. We don't always see eye to eye, but we have never had an argument or had to raise our voices to each other. I respect his opinion even if it is wrong! Love you, brother. You and your family mean the world to me.

Later in the day, a bunch of us rode over to Helen, Georgia, to have a few beers and play keno. Bob had won some money, and drinks were on him for a while.

Ended up in North Georgia the following day for their party, and Sunday I rolled to Alabama to visit Heather's grave before heading back to Dirty Jersey.

November 16, 2016. I flew out to San Antonio to attend my youngest son Dominic's graduation from boot camp in the Air Force. A longtime member and retired brother, Steve, lives there, and he picked me up at the airport and let me crash at his home for the week. He gave me his Ultra to ride for the week as well.

I attended the graduation with my ex-wife, Lucille, and her sister, Mary, who flew in from Arizona. It was a proud moment for us. He had gone from skateboards and mopeds to being a man. He would go on to do five years in the Air Force and get out in September 2021

Steve and I took a ride to Hondo, Texas, to visit our brothers Ivan (Indio), Jack, Slick, Charlie, and Wedo. I remember Steve telling me to watch out for hogs. I'm like, *What the fuck is he talking about?* Well, the ride there was pretty awesome. You ride about thirty to forty miles of just open land and ranches, then you come to a little town for about a mile or so and hit the one traffic light in it. Well, we were riding along, and I saw this big black dog trotting on the side of the rode, and I started slowing down 'cause you all know how I am with dogs. Well, Steve started screaming, "Butta, no, don't stop. It's a hog, not a dog," etc. Well, I guess we slowed to around twenty or so miles per hour as we passed this thing, and sure as shit, it took off straight for me! That's when I realized he wasn't kidding. This was like a two-hundred-pound-or-so, black-as-the-ace-of-spades hog coming straight at me!

Brother Ivan was a Wingmen extraordinaire. He is a legend and has more to do with the success and the growth of this club than just about anyone. He helped start many chapters Savannah, North Georgia, Columbus, and Calhoun County to name a few. He was a no-bullshit brother and biker. He was our national vice president for a while and was always looked upon as a leader in this club. He, Jack, Charlie, and Slick were blood brothers, and all came up in the club from very young men.

Unfortunately for Ivan, he was run off the road by a semitruck in June 2011. He was caught between the wheels of the rig and a guard rail then thrown into a swamp off the interstate exit where the accident occurred. He lost a leg and fucked up an arm to the point of possible amputation. Ivan struggled with infections and multiple operations each year since his accident up until his death in June 2020.

I am glad I got to spend this time with him at his home. He lived on an old Indian reservation that was turned into an Army fort back in the 1800s. We all came together, and their mom came over and cooked a shit ton of Mexican food for us, and we ate like kings. I had a great time that day, and it is one of my fondest memories to date in this club.

Steve and I rode back to his house in the morning, and I left Texas via airplane the next morning. Thank you, Brother Steve, for the hospitality and brotherhood. It was a trip I will always remember. Wish we lived closer, brother. Love you.

This ends my notable trips for 2016. I finished the year with 18,965 miles and visited out-of-state chapters eighteen times.

CHAPTER 18

2017

February 23, 2017. Myself, Al, Keith, and Adrian caged it to North Georgia then onto Cherokee for Carl's (Nunzi) birthday. Always a great time seeing Carl and the Jew Stogie, Coach, Vino, Aussie, and their beautiful ole ladies, Glenda, Tammi, and her royal highness, Barbra. That is a crew I definitely wish I lived closer to. As expected, Nunzi showed up a li'l before midnight. Carl, you are a great brother, and I thank you for always being there when I needed you. Love you, brother.

April 6, 2017. Jill and I headed down to Long County to spend a night with Uncle Billy and Lil Billy. Of course, it was pouring raining the whole frigging ride, but we made it there incident free.

Brother Skid played for us at the clubhouse Friday night, and it was a great time had with brothers. CC and I, of course, started a poker game which went well into the morning hours.

Saturday morning we rolled over to Uncle Billy's and met him for breakfast at the local Huddle House where he lived. Of course, there was only one cook, one waitress, and the place was slammed. So we rolled over to the McDonald's and ate there. We spent the rest of the day with Uncle Billy and Lil Billy. We crashed there for the night. First time I had to share the Scooby-Doo bunk bed with someone. I made her get on the top bunk. We rolled out at zero dark thirty and had a nice, uneventful ride home.

April 22, 2017. I headed to Slaughter Pen for their anniversary party. Wanted to see my brothers but didn't feel like staying the night, so I did a 350-mile turn and burn. I do them often to Slaughter Pen. I will ride there and meet up with brothers for lunch then jet back home. Closest chapter to us besides Rockland. Gotta show the love, but don't always want to deal with the Route 95 traffic or the added one hundred miles taking Route 81 home. So the turn and burn works for me as long as I can still do them.

May 21, 2017. Midget Steve was in our AO due to his job, and as always, he made time in his schedule to hang out with the Bergen brothers. We went to a diner and then hung out at the club house. The following morning, Keith and his then ole lady, Yvonne, had led us all to this breakfast joint over in Edgewater, New Jersey. Place was fancy, way too fancy for us for sure. Got sideways looks the whole time we were there. With fancy comes price. I think the pancakes were, like, $20!

I was glad to see Midget; we don't get to see each other too often. He lives in Iowa and drives long distance, mostly to Florida from Seattle. We speak often on the phone, and he never forgets to send me a video every year on my birthday of him singing Happy Birthday to me while driving his truck. He really helped me out with the California trip, keeping me up to date with weather and road conditions. Fucking love you, brother Midget, you sick, twisted individual.

May 24, 2017. If ever a total trip from hell, this is it. Jill and I headed to Southeast Kentucky for nationals. On the way there, we missed a deer by a couple feet who ran right out in front of us doing, like, eighty miles per hour. Then came the rain. Then two assholes decided to have some mutual road rage, and one of the assholes in an F150 just missed the ass end of Ms. Bettie by inches. He was trying to run a Honda Accord into the divider. I ended up pulling my pistol out, and they braked and continued their beef way behind us.

We had a great time in Southeast Kentucky, and the best part was, brother Jodi had brought down a sixty-foot trailer with a refer on it and put some picnic tables in the back. Yeah, I claimed my spot, and that was where I spent most of the day till the sun went down.

For those of you that haven't been able to figure it out yet, I despise the heat. Anything over sixty degrees is entirely too hot for me. I could never live down South or anywhere without a winter unless it is where I need to be either for financial or defensive purposes. I can "bear" the southwest due to the absence of humidity, but give me low thirties to fifties all day every day.

That Friday a bunch of us had taken a ride to visit Wil's grave and visit the Peacemakers MC at their clubhouse. Great time was had, and as always, outstanding hospitality from the Peacemakers MC.

Now, for the ride home, which was even more eventful than the ride there. We started off with an SUV that lost control in the middle lane at about seventy or so. The SUV swayed a few times, and everyone started braking. We were in the fast lane, about twenty-five feet behind the SUV. Then it just hung a left right into the divider right in front of us. Luckily, there was no one to the left of the vehicle, and it just did a Dale Earnhardt. I felt Jill bury her face in my back, and I braked and swerved over to the middle lane and got past the SUV before the impact pushed the vehicle back across the highway, taking out about three other vehicles. The worst for us was getting sprayed with shattering glass as we passed. We just kept on rolling.

Now for the main event! We had finally relaxed a little bit from the last incident and stopped for fuel and a bite to eat. We got back on the highway and were rolling along when I saw a black SUV sparring with an eighteen-wheel car carrier. I don't know what this truck did to the SUV, but they were pissed off, swerving at the truck and break-checking him pretty hard. I saw this and immediately went into the slow lane. Just as I got there, the SUV brake checked the truck, and he just smashed him from behind. The SUV veered off to the right and took out two other cars right in front of us while the truck hung a left at around sixty miles per hour and slammed over the divider and into oncoming traffic going south!

I got on the brakes and was mostly worried about the idiots behind us checking their Facebook accounts and not seeing what just happened in time to react. I told Jill to close her eyes and hold on (yes, we have the Sena headsets). I went off the highway, into the grass at around fifty or so miles per hour. One car had already gone off the road and past my line of travel. We were sprayed with glass, dirt, and grass, but made it through.

I looked back, and what a fucking mess. There were a few more cars that impacted each other on the northbound side that either couldn't react in time or just couldn't avoid the other cars. The real damage, though, was the southbound lanes that had the tractor trailer come across just about all lanes. I would guess at the least twenty cars and or trucks had to be involved. I eased Bettie back onto the roadway and thanked God for his hand that was upon us for sure. Made it home safe after all that.

June 9, 2017. Headed to Slaughter Pen and linked up with Damian, DT, and RB. We spent the night in the clubhouse and then headed to Moore County for their twenty-fifth anniversary party. Guess what? *It was hot as balls* 'cause, once again, I was south of the Mason–Dixon line in the fucking summer! Had a great time despite the weather, and Moore County did upgrade their AC unit, so at least inside wasn't that bad. I ended up leaving around 2100 hours Saturday night and getting home at around 0630 hours. One was to beat the heat, and two, like I've said, I'd rather deal with the deer than the morons on their phones. This would be a trend for me soon, riding more and more through the night and early mornings.

June 17, 2017. I headed down to Delray Beach to see my daughter, Mallory, and my grandson, Lewis. It was balls hot, but I will tolerate it for that little man. Spent a couple days there, going to the pool and just hanging with my prince. I then headed over to the West Coast. I was going to head up to our Central Florida chapter in Tampa to hang out with the brothers there before heading home.

I found this little place called Pine Island and decided to hang out there for the day and spend the night. I got some takeout food and rented a fishing pole from the hotel I was staying at. They had a dock in the back on a bay and ate some fish tacos while wetting a line for a while. I found a little joint up the rode and had dinner there and a few adult beverages before racking out for the night.

I got up early (I don't sleep well, ever) and hit the road when it hit me, like, sixty or so miles up the road. I left my favorite pair of

Puma sneakers in the fucking hotel room. I pulled over and called the place, and the girl said to hold on, she would check the room; of course, the kicks were gone. Man, I was pissed (1) for leaving them, and (2) why would someone want an ole pair of someone else's sneakers? I mean, these were beat the fuck up with the soles just about through and a nice hole in the top left sneaker from my shifter.

So I got back on the road, and I kept seeing this sign on Route 41 north for this place selling the "best gator bites in Florida." I want to say it was Dave's, but can't remember for sure. Anyway, I got an idea. I finally came to the joint, and it was a big-ass gas station, but not a chain one. Looked pretty worn down, but the parking lot was full with tractor trailers and pickup trucks, and it was right around lunchtime, so I figure the joint might actually have the best gator bites in Florida.

So I parked the bike and folded up my kutte and locked it in my tour pack. I pulled out my Harley windbreaker (great for when you don't want to be noticed). I grabbed my tablet case and walked inside. The place was huge inside, and right in the front a little ways past the front entrance was a huge buffet set up.

So I walked in like I owned the joint and ask loudly, "Which one of you is Dave?" This little Indian dude walked up with who I expect was his wife and let me know he was Dave. I stuck out my hand and announced myself as "Joey Butta" from YouTube Food on the Road channel. "We spoke a few days ago. I'm here to do the blog on your buffet!" He looked very perplexed and confused when his little lady took control.

"Yes, yes, of course, I remember talking to you. Yes, come and try our buffet please. Yes, yes."

She saw the free advertising opportunity way before Dave could figure it out.

They had a little chat for a moment, and you finally saw the light bulb go off in his head, then he started in with the "yes, yes, my friend, so sorry I forgot about our conversation, how was your trip here," etc. She brought me two huge plates of food with a little taste of just about everything from the buffet and a big portion of the gator bites. I asked for an orange Gatorade, and that was brought to me as well. I went over to a table and broke out my tablet and pretended to be writing something after each item of food. I was really playing poker, but hey.

I will say this, the food was top-notch, and the gator bites were pretty frigging awesome. I think they used a bunch of different curries, but doesn't matter; they were frigging awesome. I walked over to offer to pay for my meal, and they, of course, wouldn't take my money. I then purchased a ten-dollar scratch ticket. I shook their hands and thanked them and told them they would be hearing from me before the video blog aired and not to worry, I was beyond satisfied with their food! That is how you get a great free meal, brothers. Oh, I did win $50 on the scratch ticket as well. I rubbed that off at the Tampa clubhouse and bought bar cards later on that night.

Next day, myself and Mega Matt were getting on the sleds and heading over to see our brother, Shadow, who is a retired brother living a little northeast of Tampa. He had just had surgery to remove a tumor from his brain, and we wanted to pay him a visit. Now, it is never good when Mega Matt and I are left unsupervised. It took a whole, like, four minutes before we were beating some dude's ass on the side of the road for being a dick.

Long story short, we were getting on an on ramp for the interstate when this pickup slammed in front of us. His bed was full of boxes and lumber, and his tail gate was down. So he came in hot, making a left in front of us; and as he started to straighten out on the incline, a box came sliding out the truck, and it spewed like twenty-five or so small pieces of cut-up two by fours. I had plenty of room on my right and was able to get around, no issue, and excel after the dick. Mega Matt, however, took the brunt of it and had to stop and regain control of the bike. I pulled up on this idiot and told him to pull over. He did—stupid move on his part. I got to his door and laid into him and gave him a short left jab just to let him know he was a lazy piece of shit who couldn't just take the second to put up his tail gate and also didn't have to cut in front of us. Well, shame on me for just wanting to give the guy a smack to teach him a lesson and not just knock him the fuck out. He started mouthing off and got out of his truck. I slam him into the truck headfirst, and that got through to him. He was not a threat anymore; he was just running his mouth now. I told him to get in the truck and go before the bike coming up the shoulder reached him 'cause he wouldn't be as nice as I was being. I am pretty sure the dude was drunk, so I knew the cops wouldn't be called (at least not by him). Well, ole boy decided to keep running his suck, and Mega Matt got off his bike and just ran through the poor dude. It is always a thing of beauty to watch Mega Matt put in work.

We rolled into Altoona, Florida, and spent the day with brother Shadow (a.k.a. Luca Brasi). Love ya, brother. You need to get up to the dirty land for some real dirty Water Dogs!

July 22, 2017, Chopper showed time once again, and this year, it really took off. We had around fifty out-of-state brothers and most of their ole ladies show up. Saturday morning Frankie the Elbow and I took a pack of around twenty for a ride up the 9W into Upstate New York and then back down to Hank's Franks for some dirty Water Dogs. I remember we were on the 9W, and anyone who rides that road knows it is full of "Lance Armstrong" wannabes. Well, at one point, we had, like, five dudes on their ten-speeds in the middle of our pack before they started getting abused and decided it was best for them to get back in the bike lane.

August 10, 2017. I headed to Western North Carolina for the Hellbender ride. I jacked my back up on the way down and had to skip the run to the Dragon's Tail. But this trip would yield a big fruit. I met a guy who rode down with a few of his friends. His name is Zach. He originally met brother Diesel Doug a.k.a. DDD in Savannah. I believe it was St. Patty's Day weekend. He and his dad were there on vacation and rode in from Ohio. Doug invited them to the clubhouse, and the rest is history.

He began riding around three and a half hours every week from the Dayton, Ohio, area for a few months now to hang out with our Southeast Kentucky chapter. He and a few of his friends had ridden down with the SEKY crew knowing I would be present and wanted to meet me and ask what they need to do to become Wingmen and maybe have a chapter in Ohio. We didn't have a chapter in Ohio, and at the time, we only had one retired brother living up in the northern part of that state.

I sat with them and asked a lot of questions and gave little answers back to them. I told them to keep coming around and support the Wingmen and we would see what happens. Well, they took that shit as serious as a hooker relies on condoms. These guys were everywhere for the next three years.

Soon they would be known throughout our nation as the "Buckeye crew." They started conducting themselves as a chapter would: holding meetings, paying dues, vetting new guys, and writing local bylaws for themselves. They secured a "clubhouse" and were present at just about every event our nation threw from that meeting on.

Three years and five months later, the nation would finally give then the chance to stand up as a probate chapter in Ohio. They were voted on by the nation at our January 2021 national at our mother chapter in Fayetteville. They would move on to become a patched chapter of the Wingmen nation on July 25, 2021. They earned every inch of it! Very proud of those guys. SOHO in the house!

August 25, 2017. The nation had national elections, and I ran for national president unopposed. A solid brother from our Moore County chapter ran for national vice president and won the position. Johhny and I had a good relationship, and I was confident that we would work well for the good of the nation. And work we did that year! Our leadership and patience skills were put to the limits.

August 31, 2017. I headed down to North Georgia for nationals. Had a great ride down. I left Dirty Jersey around 1100 hours and got to North Georgia a little after midnight. Meeting went as planned, and North Georgia put on a great national. Ivan had come in from Texas, and the nation was excited to see him. I got to spend time with him and the Baker brothers. And got to get some good quality time in with Jack Baker; always look forward to that. I did fuck up one thing though. I had pulled out and had an awesome ride home except for one thing. I realized a couple hundred miles out, I forgot the national run flag. Luckily for me, Johhny was still there, and he secured it and took it back to Moore County with him. I am the master of the "Irish exit," and this time, it bit me in the ass.

October 20, 2017. On August 4, 2017, we lost our brother, Von Zipper. Zipper had a massive stroke a few years prior and passed due to complications. Von Zipper and I went back a long way, and I have some of my fondest and craziest memories in this club that include him. On this date, Chaz, myself, and a Bergen County hang-around named Larry rode to Moore County to pay respects to our fallen brother. And I got my run flag back.

On the ride home (Larry and I left late Saturday night; Chaz stayed and left Sunday morning), Larry and I got about fifty or so miles from the clubhouse and pulled into a gas station to fuel up. Well, tanks topped off, I started up Bettie, pulled in the clutch, dropped her into first gear, and my clutch cable snapped! Fuck my life! I noticed Larry got on his phone.

I asked him what he was doing, and he said, "Looking up hotels in the area."

I said, "Absolutely not. I am not broken down. Get behind me and push."

He looked at me like I was crazy, but I had a plan, and not getting home that night wasn't part of it. I knew if I got her running, I could power shift and get home. It was the middle of the night. No one would be on the road, and I only had to worry when stopping for fuel, which would only be two more times. I could do this! I put her in neutral, and Larry started pushing. I slammed her into first, and voilà! Larry ran back to get on his bike and catch up. I rode Bettie home without incident and got a new clutch cable a few days later.

What a trip to conclude the year for me! I rode 15,930 miles, and I visited out-of-state chapters a total of thirteen times. My lightest year since being patched out.

CHAPTER 19

2018

January 8, 2018. Flew to Tampa and then rode Mega Matt's Street Glide down to see my daughter, Mallory, and Lewis. Stayed with them for a couple of days then headed back up to Tampa to get my brother Troy's Road Glide he just got. It was a beauty. Brand-new CVO. I was humming along on Route 10 west when, all of a sudden, she just cut off. I mean, nothing—no gauges, no horn, lights, nothing. I called Northwest Florida chapter, and they were getting ready to deploy a run truck when some dude pulled over in a big-ass Ford F-350 Super Duty dually. He was dressed all proper with his khaki slacks and button-up shirt. He asked if he could help. I told him what happened, and he said he had the same bike, and it did it to him. He took the fuse cover off the box, pulled a fuse out, went to his truck, and put a new one in, and voilà! She cranked right up. I offered the guy a fifty, and he wouldn't take it. I asked him for his number; he gave me his business card. When I got home, I sent him a couple support shirts and a gift card to Amazon. I called Northwest. They spun down the blades on the bird, and off I was.

National was a good time. Of course, everyone got the Crestview crude again, and half the chapters in the nation had taken causalities. I don't know what the fuck it is about that fucking place or why we continue to hold national's there!

March 6, 2018. I had been put in touch with this guy, Larry, who lived down in South Jersey and was friends with my brother

Mike D. He was selling a 2015 Road Glide, and Mike D told me I should check it out. So I met up with the guy, and it was a beauty. He had the motor worked on, and it was pushing 107 horsepower. Motor was blacked out, and it was a sexy bike. It had five thousand miles on it! He dumped a ton of money into it, had all the receipts from Harley with the dyno sheet, etc. He told me he would take fifteen thousand for it. Now Bettie had around 202,000 miles on her, and it seemed every time I took her out, I was throwing a hundred-dollar bill at her. I sucked it up and bought the bike and retired Bettie to just the East Coast runs. And so my days of owning Road Glides had begun.

April 13, 2018. Hang-around Larry was now a prospect. He and I had gotten on the road and headed down to Fayetteville for our brother Lo's memorial. Lo had passed due to injuries from a wreck he had on December 21, 2017. Lo was a great brother and a man of few words. When he did talk, you wanted to listen. He was biker through and through. He and his ole lady had recently moved to Tampa and were living the dream on the river. Much love and respect, brother Lo. How "Lo" can you go?

May 21, 2018. Headed to Northeast Georgia for national that was hosted by Northeast Georgia and our Dawson County chapters.

Now, on the way down, it was the fucking devil's furnace. I mean stupid hot, and I was miserable. I decided to stop and get a room right outside Charlotte. Well, I found this little Haji joint that was just enough of a dump for my liking and walked inside to get a room. I asked for a smoking room with any type of bed on the first floor. He said, "No problem," and asked for my license and credit card. I asked him how much the room was, and he said $225! I don't know if it was the heat or the fact that this motherfucker just insulted my intelligence, but I just fucking snapped. I grabbed him and body-slammed him on the counter and asked him if he thought I was a retard or something. He started screaming about the holiday and being close to the airport. Well, I don't know how he got there so fast or who called him, but I heard tires screeching and looked to the parking lot, and coming in hot was a black-and-white. I grabbed Haji and brought him in close and told him it was a misunderstanding and if he got me cuffed, I'd make sure one day his place was a pile of ashes with him and his family in it.

So the "officer" came in, hand on gun, and asked if there was a problem. I really wanted to ask him how the fuck he knew to pull in here but decided better of it. I mean, seriously, I had Haji by the collar for maybe thirty seconds, and boom, here's Johnny! I told him that the owner of the very nice establishment and I just had some words of disagreement about the price and that I was just leaving. He looked over at Haji and he nodded in agreement. Then the gang member asked me if I was leaving Charlotte as well. I told him, of course; if I couldn't stay here, I didn't want to slum it and would just be on my way to the next town. He offered to follow me to the interstate. What a guy! Fucking dick.

I rolled around another fifty or so miles and got a room with a much nicer and understanding Haji owner.

Meetings went well, and all had a great time. I love when I get to spend time with my Dawson brother, Bob, and get to see his family.

We had some brothers who had either moved to Huntsville or were hitting the roads there from our Calhoun County chapter that were asking the nation to probate a chapter there. Hence, the Rocket City chapter from Huntsville was taking off for flight. Brothers Walt, Weird Al, Tom, Johhny "Pain," and Steve Rust put in some work, and it was paying off. They got the vote, and HVAL was up and running.

Poured the whole way home. I caught up to the Bergen brothers at a gas stop in Virginia. They had left earlier than I did. Ms. Bettie was slipping and sliding all over the road; the rear tire was at the end of its life. I told Al I would just pull out ahead of them since they were stopping to eat. Well, I hit the on-ramp and started banging gears, hit a paint strip and spun the rear tire, and the front end went into a wobble. I wasn't worried so much if I dumped her since there was so much water I would slide it out. I was worried about the idiots not paying attention and getting run over. I got off the throttle and leaned into the handlebars with just about all I had, and slowly she came back under control. It was then I noticed a pickup truck behind me swerving back and forth, slowing down oncoming traffic.

The guy pulled alongside me and asked if I was good. I nodded and shouted a thank-you and rolled on.

June 7, 2018. I headed down to Long County for their anniversary party. I stopped by and stayed at CC's house that Thursday night. He and his wife had just had a little baby girl, and I was asked to be her godfather. We hung out, did some fishing in his backyard, and just enjoyed some quiet R and R.

Friday morning Lil Mike, Hayden, and I rolled out to see Uncle Billy and Lil Billy and have breakfast with them. We hung out with Uncle Billy for a while then headed back to Long County's clubhouse for the party.

August 24, 2018. The nation voted Stew (my then national sergeant at arms) as our new national vice president. Johhny Moffit did not run again, as his duties as an active member in the Army came and snatched him from us for a while. Johnny is a great Wingmen and did a great job as our national vice president. He also is a great soldier, and that is where he needed to be for the time being. Thank you, Johhny, for your hard work and dedication. Sapper thanks, you two! Stew was my national sergeant, and he stepped up to the plate. I ran unopposed again.

August 31, 2018. Rode down to Fayetteville for my thirty-sixth consecutive national. Fayetteville went old-school and had the event on a big ole piece of property with a huge barn on it. I didn't mind the old-school, but dammit, man, it was, like, 105 degrees with 100 percent humidity! And the lighting sucked in the barn. Food was killer, and the brotherhood was awesome. We ended up getting a great club photo and video of a very good portion of the nation on the highway four wide and very deep.

September 29, 2018. Myself, Igor, Mark "SK," and prospect Jon "Gas Cap" headed down to Slaughter Pen for Jon's first out-of-state run. Jon is the son of a longtime supporter of ours, Joe Banasi. He is young and has brought a younger outlook and appeal to the Bergen chapter. Jon did great on the run. He had an older Softail at the time and has since moved up to the Road Glide mafia. It is good to watch the boy become a man. Very proud of you, brother Gas Cap.

October 4, 2018. Decided to ride out to our Devil's Elbow chapter and spend some quality time with brother Stew. Stew and I go back to my prospecting days and he has been there for me through thick and thin 100 percent of the time. He is a true brother and Wingmen.

Stew spent most of his young and adult life in the Army, reaching the rank of command sergeant major. He recently retired, and like all military retirees, he decided to work! WTF? He bought a chunk of land and decided to build a farm and raise pigs, goats, chickens, and some other animals. His place has got it all: pasture, secluded, pond, etc. We spent a few days riding and just chilling on his farm and visiting the local VFW for some adult beverages with the local veterans. I had a great time with a great brother.

October 26, 2018. I rode down to our Beaufort chapter to celebrate brother Super Dave's thirtieth anniversary as a Wingmen!

That Friday morning, I hooked up with brother Lil Dwayne from Savannah for lunch and just riding around Savannah. Ended up at the Harley dealer 'cause my throttle grip had slipped the gear, and I had no throttle. Went and saw Brooke at the dealer, and as always, she hooked me up, and I had a new throttle assembly to get me going again.

That night I had an awesome time; as always, it's good to hang with Animal, Artie, Todd, and Big Happy! Love you, brothers, and love you, Super Dave. Thank you for your decades of giving to this club and paving the way for the next generations of Wingmen.

This concludes my memorable runs for 2018. I rode a total of 17,466 club miles and visited out-of-state chapters ten times.

CHAPTER 20

2019

January 17, 2019. I flew into Savannah and rented a car (due to weather) and headed down to see my daughter, grandson, and new granddaughter, Cecilia! I spent a few days there then drove up to Central Florida Tampa chapter then up to Jacksonville, North Carolina, for nationals.

I got there on Wednesday night. That Thursday Sapper and I were riding around town (he had given me his chopper to ride). I also had a meeting set up with another club who had become a thorn in my side over the last few years. Their new national president wanted to meet and try to work things out. We had been playing ping-pong with them for a while now.

Funny, they had some guys from out of state hiding out in a tattoo parlor. Sapper and I had gone there so I could get my CC tattoo in honor of my granddaughter. You should have seen the looks on their faces when we rolled up. I just looked and said, "I bet I know why you guys are in town." They shuffled out and headed up the road. We had the meeting. Nothing changed. Another case of wanting to dress the part and look cool, but don't think following MC protocol applies. It's cool. Ping-pong is a fun game.

I drove the rental back to Savannah and sat in that fucking airport for thirteen hours. I would've left and went to the clubhouse or a brother's house, but they kept telling us the flight would leave in an hour or forty-five minutes. Brutal trip, but I had to fly due to it being hurricane season which, of course, brought in a hurricane. Jacksonville had, like, eight inches of water on the property that weekend.

February 28, 2019. Larry and I had decided to ride down to Effingham for a party. Well, we left and hit the 95 south, and it was, like, twenty-five degrees. No problem. Our heated gear was powered up, and we were comfortable. Well, the sun dropped out (we left after work), and it went into the teens. We were in lower Virginia, and it started freezing rain mixed with snow. We were fine. We got this. We had ridden in worse! Well, we pulled off the 95 to fuel up, and as we were fueling, a couple of snowplows went by, and it was getting worse. We looked at each other and laughed and said, "Fuck it. Let's press on." We got back on the 95, and now it was snowing like nobody's business. We pulled off and decided to get a Haji special. Larry put his brand-spanking-new tampon cover on his bike. I, of course, made fun of him for it. We grabbed a bite to eat and racked out.

We got up around 0500 hours, and there was around four inches of snow on the ground! I was not laughing at Larry anymore after he removed the tampon cover and his bike was nice and dry while mine was covered in snow and ice! We decided to head back home since the weather was actually worse south of us. Larry got me a tampon cover a week or so later. It's always in my tour pack now. Thank you, brother. Love ya.

March 22, 2019. Larry and I headed down to our Beaufort chapter to pay respects to our fallen brother, Luis, and attend his memorial party.

A while back, Mega Matt had left the Wingmen nation and had since become a Warlock in Florida. Matt and I were and still are very close. I won't fault a brother for leaving if he thinks he is going to do something that he thinks is a better fit for him. There were a lot of issues with Mega Matt and the chapter he was in, and he made a decision to leave.

A week or so prior, "Grub," the founder of the Warlock's MC, passed. Grub was an MC icon, and I decided to go and attend his funeral out of respect to him and get a chance to see Mega Matt.

So myself, Roundy, CC, Larry, Scuba Steve, and Johhny Moffit headed up to Lexington, South Carolina, and pay our respects. It was great to see Mega Matt and shoot the shit with him. I love that brother and will till the wheels fall off. RFFDD.

On the ride back to Beaufort, we all stopped for dinner. In conversation, Larry was talking about how he and I have ridden a lot of miles together, and where you see Butta, you see Larry. Roundy then said, "Kinda like Butta is on Toast." Hence, Larry got his road name, Toast.

Larry and I took off zero dark thirty Sunday morning. We were rolling along up the 95, making great time. We got to the Quantico area (basically Slaughter Pen), and Bettie went in a wobble. I knew right away what happened 'cause it has happened before. She blew the rear wheel bearing. Larry pulled in behind me and started going to the right shoulder. I kept going at around fifty miles per hour. He saw this and sped up alongside me and looked at me like, "What the fuck?" I shouted to him, "I blew the rear wheel bearing!"

He said, "Okay, well, let's pull over."

Now this is where I just fucking lost it and was so over Ms. Bettie taking a shit every time she was anywhere near Slaughter Pen.

I yelled back, "No, I am not fucking breaking down here. We will make it home!"

Larry didn't know what to do, so he fell in behind me just as the rear wheel hub exploded! He was hit with all kinds of fucking shrapnel in the face, arms, and chest. We finally pulled over, and I was pissed. I love this bike, but to be honest, I wanted to light her on fire. We decided to get off the highway. There was an exit like a quarter mile up the road. Well, Larry went to pull off the shoulder and get the slow lane for me when an eighteen-wheeler decided to abruptly pull into the same lane, doing, like, seventy miles per hour. If Larry's front tire had a little more thread on it, he would've gotten hit!

We made it to a gas station, and we called brother Eclipse. He sent the Calvary over to the rescue. Brothers Eclipse, DT, and ET showed up with in thirty minutes with a truck, trailer, and a Street Glide for me to ride home. Larry and I made it home, and that little stunt of being a stubborn ass cost me a rear rim as well. Eclipse rode Bettie up to Delaware to swap out bikes a week later. Love you, brother. You always have my back!

April 25, 2019. Myself, Jill, Keith, Toast, and his ole lady, Danielle, headed to Huntsville. Rocket City! We all had a great time there, and we did the tourist thing going to the NASA museum and all the space stuff in town.

We had been invited by the Legacy Vets MC to attend a barbecue that Saturday as well. While we were there, Walt, the president of our Huntsville chapter, got a call that one of our out-of-state prospect's ole lady had shot herself in the ass! Yes, you read that correctly. She shot herself in the ass. Apparently, she was in the head, and when she pulled her pants down, her sidearm—which was waist holstered—either fell and discharged or the trigger got hung up and discharged. Either way, she shot herself in the ass! She took it like a trooper, and the jokes and T-shirt ideas began to fly!

May 30, 2019. Jill and I headed down to Phenix City for nationals. Had a great ride down, and it really wasn't too hot for once on the ride. It was ass-crack-sweat hot down there however!

Had a great national meeting and went to dinner Saturday night with a bunch of brothers and their ole ladies. Hit up some local bars and got to hang out with my favorite redheaded hooker brother, Finch. Had a great ride back weather wise and without incident, a rare treat for sure.

June 28, 2019. Headed to Dawson County to check out the new piece of property and clubhouse they just bought. I stayed with brother Vino and his beautiful wife, Tami. Thank you for the hospitality, brother. Always love hanging with you guys.

Saturday myself, Cory, Finch, Tom, Bob, Jew Bear, and a prospect rolled down to Unadilla, Georgia, to check out Angel City Campgrounds. We were thinking of hosting a national party there. Well, when I tell you it was hot, it was stupid-hooker-sweating-in-church-while-stealing-money-from-the-donation-plate hot!

We walked around with the owner of the joint for an hour or so and then headed out. We all stopped to get something to eat then headed out to our separate destinations.

Well, Finch, Tom and I were riding together up 85. They would break off from myself at the north side of Hotlanta, and I would continue on home from there. Well, this is why I shouldn't own a bike with a lot of motor work done to it. We were kicking it 100, 110 the whole way. I got home, and the Road Glide was put away, ridden hard and wet.

July 5, 2019. Jill and I head to Fayetteville for their annual Fourth of July party and the club's fortieth anniversary party. The joint was packed, and Fayetteville put on a great weekend. Walter and Coup had the grills going, and everyone had a great time. Of course, it was hot as balls.

July 26, 2019. I headed down to Long County with Jill for CC's fiftieth birthday party. I think this is the party when he got fucked up and decided to shave his hair into a Mohawk. Hey, we all deal with midlife crisis in our own way, I guess. Lil Mike owed up on a bet he and I had made that Alabama college football team would have a better record than the Georgia Bulldogs. Roll Tide, they didn't disappoint. Mike had to wash Ms. Bettie, and a fine job he did!

July 30, 2019. It was Bergen's chopper show once again, and a shitload of brothers had showed up. Two of my favorite brothers, Finch my Red Hooker and Tom "Not My Real Name" Smith, showed up. We were out tooling around all day. They had taken a ride down to my house to let my dogs out and feed them with me.

Now a week or so before, I had taken the Road Glide to the dealer 'cause she was spitting some smoke. They called that day and told me the front rings were fried and that, most likely, I'd be getting a new motor through the warranty. We decided to roll over there on our way back to the clubhouse, and I decided to make a deal on a 2019 Road Glide special with the 114-inch motor that will now be considered a leftover the following day. Bergen Harley did me right as they always do, and the deal was done, and I picked it up the following week. I paid 15,000 for the 2015 Road Glide, and they gave me 16,500 for it, knowing the warranty will take care of the motor.

August 12, 2019. Larry, Gas Cap, myself, and the ole ladies pulled a turn and burn to Slaughter Pen for lunch with the Virginia brothers. It was nice to see Doc Kipp. He works like a redheaded whore in the circus, and I don't get to see him as often as I would like to. We all had a great lunch on the Potomac River, then the Bergen crew headed up the 95 back home. It was my first real milage ride on the new Road Glide. I was very impressed.

August 28, 2019. Headed down to Beaufort for nationals. Had a great ride down, and for once, it wasn't too hot going, being there or coming home. Don't get to say that too often while visiting Beaufort.

Thursday I spent the day with Sapper. We hit some island and had an awesome lunch at some little shack selling all kinds of seafood. We were there for hours, eating and shooting the shit.

Friday I met up with Albie and had lunch with him and a few adult beverages. Same thing, just sitting around, eating good food, and having good conversation. Those are sometimes the best times.

I had the honor at the meeting with presenting Mike Roy, one of our founding fathers, with his thirty-year active pin. Mike has been an inspiration to us all. Still crushing the miles after all these years. When Mike was younger in the club, he was active Army and lost some active time due to his commitment to the Army. Hence, the thirty-year pin through the club was on forty years.

I was supposed to head down to Delray Beach to see my grandkids and have a meeting with a national president of a club down there, but Hurricane Dorian decided to smack the shit out of Florida and was heading up the coast. I canceled and rode home. The next morning (August 2), my wife and I jumped on the bike and took a ride up to Ithaca New York, to the Finger Lakes. If you have never been to Ithaca, enter at your own risk! Beautiful place to see and ride the roads. Lakes, waterfalls, forests, tons of shit to do and see. All that aside, there is one exception that makes it suck. It is a college town, and it is a liberal-as-fuck place to go. Bunch of wannabe, hippie, rich White kids fighting for every right on the planet except a good one for the country. Bunch of snowflake, moronic, whiny little douchebags who have nothing better to do than point fingers and blame everyone else for their problems. Enough said, or I will never finish this book.

From Ithaca, we went home. I got a good night's sleep. I awoke and kissed my wife and dogs, and off to the left coast I headed. I always wanted to ride to California and back just to do it. So that was what I set off to do.

So on September 5 I did just that. Loaded up the Road Glide and headed to the base of the George Washington Bridge then started going west. I have to tell you, I did this round trip in eight days. I have never in my life been so lucky with weather. It was incredible. I ended up putting on rain gear one time for around three hours in the middle of Wyoming. Other than that, it was long-sleeve T-shirt or wifebeater and kutte the whole trip.

I stopped the first night at the Ohio/Indiana border. Then rolled through to the middle of Nebraska for the second night. I rolled into Cheyenne, Wyoming the next day and had an appointment to get my five-thousand-mile service done. I pulled out of there late afternoon, and a few hours later is when I hit the rain. I rode for a few hours and decided to stop at the western end of Wyoming for the night 'cause of the rain and lightning. I stopped in Little America, Wyoming. I got a room and headed over to the truck stop to get some dinner. I ended up at a table with four truck drivers who were just sitting around, eating, and telling tall tales. It was a good time.

Next morning I was back on the road, and when I got to the Salt Flats in Utah, I decided to stop and take some pictures. It is an incredible sight to see. There was a rest area with restrooms and a couple of food trucks. A lot of people were walking around on the Salt Flat, which looks like a big-ass lake covered in snow.

I walked over to the head and noticed an old Indian man with a table set up, selling jewelry. I walked over and decided to get something for my wife and myself. The old man struck up a conversation with me and asked where I was coming from. I told him, New Jersey. I told him I had always wanted to go coast to coast just to say I did it.

He then asked me if I believe in God, and I answered, "Yes, I do." Then he asked me if I would pray with him over my bike for it and I to have a safe and knowledgeable journey. I said, "Of course, I would be honored." I helped him walk over, and we prayed together. He told me he was Navajo Indian and then said a prayer in his native language.

Now, I am a big believer in God and have my own ways of talking to him multiple times a day. I'm not big on churches and paying a percentage of my income to God. The memorable words of Bono, "The God I believe in isn't short of cash!" Anyway, what I am trying to say is, it was a very powerful and spiritual moment, praying with that man I had just met maybe twenty minutes before.

I helped him back to his chair, and I picked out a necklace for my wife, and I picked out a Lady Madonna necklace to wear and keep on the bike. We were just talking again, and he asked if I minded if he ate while we talked. I told him, "Of course not." He opened this old brown paper bag that looked like it had been used a couple of hundred times and pulled out this big sandwich. He told me it was peanut butter and black raspberry jelly with honey. All homemade by his wife on home-baked bread. He then laughed and told me my eyes were telling him I was hungry and pulled the sandwich apart and handed me half of it. We sat there for about another hour before I took off. I can't even begin to be able to pronounce his name, and though I wanted to so badly, I did not ask to take a picture with him 'cause the whole time we were sitting together, talking, a lot of the tourists were looking at and buying jewelry and taking pictures of the both of us. I guess it was probably a sight to see the old Indian guy and the not-as-old biker in his kutte. Anyway, I didn't want to water the moment down to a tourist-type thing.

The old man and I shook hands, and he gave me an embrace, not a hug, I mean an embrace—there is a big difference. You could tell he meant it. He wished me well and to have a safe trip home. He thanked me for the company and conversation. I got on the bike and headed west again.

I made it to California and went over the Golden Gate Bridge. I had lunch at a Russian Deli in San Francisco, then I walked into the Pacific Ocean with my boots on. Then I rode down the coast to Santa Cruz. That is when I had just enough of the California coast, so I headed inland and spent the night in Bakersfield. Then in the morning, I started banging miles back toward home.

I did the trip in a total of eight days and seven nights. I rode 6,332 miles. It was one of the best things I've decided to do in my life. When I returned home, I wrote this and passed it on to my brothers.

This trip I've taken has been a very humbling experience. Anyone who doesn't believe in God or a higher power, you need to do something like this to be able to see everything that's been created across this beautiful country to give us the power and resources to be the greatest country in the world. It's pretty amazing stuff. I don't care if you believe in our Lord and Savior, Jesus Christ, or Buddha or Zeus. There is definitely something else higher than all science can try to prove that created this earth without a doubt. I don't include Allah because I believe he is a fake mythical creature. I have witnessed the birth of my children. I have two grandchildren. I have been reborn into the Wingmen nation. I have had my heart broken, and I have broken many hearts. This trip is right up there with all my top life events. It's an exhilarating feeling, being all by yourself, traveling over three thousand miles one way and turning around and coming back. The sights I have witnessed, the magnificent spectacles that God has created, the people I've met along the way. From sharing a dinner table with some truckers in Wyoming or just saying hello and chitchatting in a gas station. I met a Navajo Indian in Utah who prayed over my bike for a safe journey. He shared his homemade peanut-butter-and-jelly sandwich his wife made him with me. This was a great spiritual experience. I reached out to my brothers Mike Roy and Robbie Goodman at one point to try to explain what I was feeling. They are the most spiritual men I know. I knew they would understand. I definitely need to do this more often. I went over the Appalachian Mountains, the Rocky Mountains, and the Sierra Mountains. Both continental divides over the San Rafael Bridge and Golden Gate Bridge. I walked on the Bonneville Salt Flats and put my feet in the Great Salt Lake of Utah and the Pacific Ocean. I rode the Pacific Coast Highway and through the high plain desert of California and the Mojave desert. I rode through towns that many of my favorite songs were written about. I saw wild horses, an elk, and a rattlesnake! Some said I'm crazy for doing this alone. Some said I should've taken more time. I say, I listened to what was going on inside me and followed my instinct. I wouldn't change anything.

If you haven't done something like this, *do it!* However you see fit. Best thing I've done in a long time. Love and respect, Joey "Butta" NP WMC WFFW RFFDD.

That concluded my most memorable trips for 2019. What a way to finish out the year. I rode 24,526 miles with my kutte on my back and visited out-of-state chapters twelve times. I rode through a total of twenty-eight states.

CHAPTER 21

2020: The Year of the COVID-19!

January 18, 2020. Bergen County hosted the national, and the weather cooperated for the most part. It did snow for around ten minutes, causing me to lose a bar card bet to my brother Roy Willey. The meeting and party were all good, and Al kept everyone fat and happy as usual. My daughter, Melissa, was the recipient of the Sid scholarship award from Dawson County, and she got to be present at the beginning of the meeting to receive her check.

February 27, 2020. Chaz and I drove to Oak Grove chapter for their anniversary party. I got to hang out with brother Rico, which is always something to look forward to. We were also patching out "Frost" from our Southeast Kentucky chapter. We waited till after midnight so his official patch date would be February 29, 2020. Now he won't receive a year star till the next leap year! WASH THAT CIVILIAN STINK OFF YOU, BOY! Love ya, brother.

May 18, 2020. I headed out to our Oak Grove chapter to meet up with the national president of another club and handle some business. Eclipse had hooked up with me to stand in for one of my national sergeant of arms. I decided to make him one of my national sergeant of arms after his show of dedication and wiliness to put in work at the drop of a dime. If you're not willing to say yes, I will be there without hesitation. That position or any position isn't for you. Just saying. Eclipse never hesitated or tried to rearrange any task given, ever. Hard work pays off.

From Oak Grove, Eclipse and I headed to Huntsville, where we separated so he could go and surprise his sons. I rode on to Calhoun County and went to visit Heather's grave for her birthday. I then continued on to Phenix City, where I hooked up with brother Gabe, and together we headed down to Enterprise, Alabama, and met up with Big Steve, Crazy Joe "Hulk" Hernandez, Damion, Clay "Tilt," and Johnny Velcro. We all ended up at the town dive bar and got some eats and drinks till wee hours of the morning. I crashed at Big Steve's house and hit the road early, with Gabe back up to Cherokee County for our first ever COVID national.

We limited the meeting to just presidents to try and minimize the emanate casualties of COVID. This meeting one of my favorite brothers was expelled from the club, Lil Mike. It broke my heart, but his actions had become an issue with the club, and he was heading down a road of repeat that didn't look like he would be able to exit from for the long haul. This was a case of repeat offending. I hope his life turns around and he becomes the man we all knew in the beginning.

The ride home was a good: one, the weather held up, and the best was, the roads were clear as fuck due to most states being shut down by a bunch of pussies who say they are for the good of America. You know, due to the virus that was created in a lab in China, funded by Bill Gates and the Obama administration, and released on the world by the Chinese government.

Anyway, I was on the road for six days and visited six chapters and road 3,003 miles. Fuck you, COVID.

July 8, 2020. Jill and I packed up the RV and threw the dogs in and headed down to Southeast Kentucky. We were around four or five hours out and decided to stop for the night in a rest area and sleep. The dogs didn't sleep much or allow us to. They barked at every car door or voice. We had gotten there and set up shop in a small RV park a couple miles from the clubhouse. Brother Curtis let us use his Ultra Classic, so Jill and I got some much-needed R and R and riding that Saturday. We hit a couple of flea markets and yard sales and had a really good time just riding around. The dogs did well. We only had two dogs then: Lilia, our English Lab, and Loki, our golden retriever puppy.

We headed back north and found an RV park in upper West Virginia to stop for the night. It was right on a river, and Lilia went in, and her Lab instincts took over, and she was like a fish. She gave us a look like, "Why have you never done this with me before?" We made it home, and our first trip ever in an RV was a success. It would definitely start an itch that we would scratch, hard.

August 14, 2020. I blasted down to North Georgia for Ivan's memorial. Got to hang out with Uncle Billy and CC there. A lot of the nation showed up to pay respects to Ivan as they should have. I ended up having to bolt out of there early Saturday morning 'cause my boss had called me on a bluff and told me he needed me to work on Sunday. Remember, I work for the state, and my state being a part of the Northeast Communist Bloc of the United States means, if I don't follow the governor's rules, I can lose my job. My boss had asked me where I was going when I put in for a vacation day for that Friday, and I told him to "suck a fat baby's dick, it's none of your business." He reminded me of the governor's "mandates" and told me he didn't want to see me getting jammed up, being caught out of state (he, of course, knows how much I travel since he signs off on my time-off papers). I told him I was staying home to work on my RV.

Well, Saturday morning Stew and I were having breakfast at the great Waffle House when he called me and told me mandatory overtime Sunday morning at 0600 hours. He was waiting for me to grovel and come up with an excuse 'cause he knew damn well I was not in New Jersey. Well, I called his bluff as well and just calmly said, "Great. I need the overtime. Thanks, Boss!" Touché!

Well, I scoffed down my "all-star breakfast" and returned to the hotel, packed my shit, and dee-deed out of Georgia. Of course, I got about a hundred miles out, and the skies opened up! I rode the rest of the eight hundred and change miles in the rain, but I made it home in thirteen hours and got plenty of sleep before going to work Sunday morning with a smile. I knew he was just testing me, so I sat in the shop for eight hours 'cause there was no emergency job!

August 31, 2020. Both Stew and I ran unopposed for national president and national vice president. This coming term would be my fifth and last.

September 2, 2020. My good friend of over ten years, Ox, had decided to stand up again and try prospecting for the nation again. He had done so some years ago and stood down due to his priorities with a new family and career. Ox had stayed in touch with many brothers throughout the nation and traveled to many events over the years between then and now. I was glad he was finally in the right place to try to become a Wingmen. He had a guy, "Dyna" Johhny, who had been coming around as well and was also showing interest in standing up. They had been hanging around for a few months now.

Well, I was heading down to our Western North Carolina chapter for nationals and to run the Dragon's Tail with some brothers that were all meeting down there on Thursday and Friday to do some riding. I told them they should come.

Going to a national as a hang-around gives you a better perspective of what you are getting yourself into, and vice versa. We get to see you as you and not a prospect just eager to please.

I always take a hang-around out of state before they stand up 'cause I want to see what they got in the seat as well. Now Ox had ridden with me many times, but I didn't know this Johhny guy from atom, so off we went.

We got to around Richmond, Virginia, on the 95, and the skies opened up. We held up for the night in a Haji special I got us and continued on in the morning. Now, mind you, they have to stop when I stop, they have to go when I go, and best yet, they have to eat when and what I eat! Ox hates McDonald's and I, if I stop, eat McDonald's every time on the road for breakfast. Sausage McMuffin with egg, hash browns, and an orange drink. Five minutes. Boom, back on the bike. Usually the only meal I eat. I will have a few snickers bars and some beef jerky on the bike to munch on after that.

We rolled into Western, and there were a lot of brothers around. Ox and Johhny got a good reception, and a bunch of us headed up to the Dragon's Tail. Brother Curtis "Ray Donovan" from Western was leading the pack with me since he knew where we were going.

We rode the tail twice, then a bunch of us stopped at a local joint and had lunch and a few beers. We shot the shit and told tall tales of days gone by.

Brother Curtis impressed the shit of me that day with his riding skills. Yes, he has the home-field advantage of riding those roads all the time, but damn, he can ride. Dyna Johhny impressed me as well; he did great on the ride down, and he and that little Dyna were crushing it on the tail.

Saturday we held the second COVID national, and it was a big day. We were welcoming two new chapters into the nation that day. Southeast Georgia and South Alabama chapters were awarded their charters!

September 18, 2020. Ox and Johhny were stood up and now official prospects for the Wingmen nation. I was happy they both decided to stand up. Johhny seemed to be eager to learn and was a young pipe hitter, and Ox and I have been close friends for around a decade. I know that relationship would only grow if he were to be a Wingmen as well. And so their journey begins.

October 9, 2020. Prospect Ox, myself, and Jill rolled down to Slaughter Pen. Brother Robo's kid, Cody, had stood up some time back, and tonight was his big night. I know Cody since he was like six or seven. It is pretty cool to watch him go from a BMX bike to a prospect getting patched out by his father who is now also his president.

A lot of out-of-state brothers showed up for the event, and I know it was one of brother Robo's proudest moments.

That Saturday I was hanging in DT's toy hauler, getting some ink from brother Levi. I had gotten a comet for my golden retriever, Comet, who had recently passed, and I got "Don't die today" on my forearm to help fend off the grim reaper on a daily basis. Well, brother Sapper was in for the event, and this motherfucker was so stoned and had us pissing with the shit coming out of his brain. Fucking love you, Sapper.

November 6, 2020. Prospect Ox and I headed down to our Little River chapter for a special national executive council meeting. It was fucking cold, but the heated gear made it a pretty comfortable ride for the most part.

We had our meeting and got shit taken care of and then hung out at the Little River clubhouse. I got to see brothers Randy "Daddio" and Flounder, two brothers I don't get to see enough for sure. We hung around and shot the shit over some beers, Ox got to meet some of the old-timers in the club and got to listen and learn. Lee had come down to hang with us after he got off work in Fayetteville, and he and Ox got some good face time in. Ox and Lee had kept in touch from back in the day with Ox's first go-around.

This concludes my most memorable rides for the year 2020. I ended the year with 9,406 miles. I visited out-of-state chapters ten times.

This was my lowest milage year by far, and brother Larry Toast had unseated my thirteen-consecutive-year run on highest miles in my chapter. I have been slowing down and hadn't been getting out on the road as much as I had been. I had the feeling of burning out, and I noticed I wasn't enjoying the ride as much as I have in the past. It is for these reasons I decided that 2021 would be my last year as national president, and I would not run for the position again.

CHAPTER 22

2021

January 15, 2021. Prospect Ox and I headed down to Fayetteville for national. I wanted my last January national as national president to be at our mother chapter. It was pretty cold, but this was Ox's first national run as a prospect, and I wanted to ride side by side with him.

The nation voted on standing up the Southern Ohio chapter for probate status. Very proud moment for those guys. They had put in so much work already, and now they finally got their chance to prove themselves Wingmen worthy.

I had a plaque made for Larry Toast. A passing of the torch, I knew he wasn't going to slow down anytime soon, and I definitely was. Larry has that magic mix that I was fortunate to have: great job that affords tons of time off, the fortitude to ride hard, and an ole lady who understands. He would now be Bergen's human run flag. I am proud of your commitment to the club and our brothers. Love ya, brother. Nothing but "Scotch and regret" from here on out! Make it count.

February 19, 2021. Prospect Ox and I headed out to Southern Ohio to check in on the new probate chapter. We caged it due to snow and freezing rain the whole way.

Their clubhouse was coming along, and the probates were all eager to learn the Wingmen way. A few out-of-town brothers showed up as well, and a good time was had by all. I couldn't wait for the opportunity to ride there; the area was really nice. Lots of farmland and open roads.

April 15, 2021. Prospect Ox and I headed to Southeast Kentucky. I had to meet some of my council there and tend to a situation. All went well, and we all as a pack headed up to Southern Ohio. On the ride into Kentucky, I forgot what highway we were on, but we were cruising along at about eighty miles per hour when I noticed something in the road ahead as we came over a rise in the road. Well, we came up on it pretty quick when I noticed it was Bambi! A decent-sized spike just standing broadside right in the middle of the highway. I braked hard, as did Ox. It finally walked very nonchalantly in front of Ox and then toward our direction. I swear, if Ox wanted to, he could've pet it on his way past. I noticed, like, four or five more deer on the right shoulder. It was like this dude was dared to go out there and play chicken, and they were watching him.

Ohio was having a barbecue and just hosting some brothers, and a bunch of locals in the area showed up to check out the Wingmen MC that had just moved into their area. Some of the brothers hit some of the local bars, and a great time was had by all. Doc Jason and I did a little "shopping" while we were there and got some really great deals.

Later in the day, I presented bottom rockers to the probates that had earned the right to wear them. It was a good trip all around.

May 2, 2021. Bergen County was having our "spring breakout run." We do it every year usually in April to make sure all the members bikes are up to par for the upcoming riding season.

We decided (well, Keith decided) to go to a bar/restaurant in the Poconos just over the Pennsylvania border. We were saddling up, and RB was still fucking with his new Bluetooth helmet. There were around ten or elven of us total. Well, Al and Keith were up front, and I guess they thought everyone was leg over and ready to go, so they took off, and everyone followed, except me. I was waiting for RB, and he was pissed 'cause they weren't paying attention and left us. So now he went into full RB mode and was just taking his sweet-ass time.

I finally said, "You know, we can still catch up, brother. I don't know where this place is, but I know the general direction they will be going."

"Fuck this. Fuck them. I'm going to Mare's!"

So I dropped her into first and started riding like I rented it to try to catch the pack. I caught up about ten or so miles on Route 80 and pulled up to the front and told them RB wouldn't be making the trip.

We got to this joint, and I have to say, Keith does know his food joints. It was on the Delaware River, and the food was really good. I remember the Thai garlic wings were awesome. I broke off after food and drinks since living in Central Jersey now it wasn't necessary to go back to the clubhouse or in that general direction. I blasted down some nice back roads and had a great ride back home.

May 26, 2021. Prospect Ox and I headed down the 95 to visit our new Southeast Georgia chapter. We would then head to Savannah for nationals. Now a couple weeks prior, I was woken in the middle of the night with the feeling of someone sticking a very large knife in my right kidney. After an hour or so of rolling on the floor in agony, I agreed to let my wife take me to the hospital. Remember, New Jersey was still thinking COVID is going to kill the planet. She couldn't come in with me, so I dragged my ass in and told the woman at the emergency room desk, "Pretty sure I got kidney stones. Get me drugs now!"

She was awesome. All she wanted was my ID and INS card. She got security to put me in a wheelchair, and she admitted me while he took me in the back. Some doctor came asked me, like, two questions about the pain and where it was then spiked me with some narcotic. About three minutes later, I was telling her how much I loved her and she could have everything I owned.

So prognosis is, three stones in the kidney, and one decided to move. Pain meds followed up with urologist, and home I went.

Now back to the trip. We rolled to Southeast and got to the clubhouse. I was literally bent over on my tank; my kidney hurt so bad. I got to hang out with Scuba Steve and a few other brothers, then CC, myself, and Ox headed over to where brother Cowboy from Long County lived. Larry Toast and his ole lady had rented a cabin, and they were all throwing a barbecue. Brother Country and his ole lady were there, along with brother Rob Mas and his ole lady. Larry was cooking, and beer and drinks were plentiful. It was a good time. However, my kidney was killing me, I ended up leaving early to go on to Savannah and get situated in my room and take some pain meds.

The Savannah chapter, as I have mentioned, always kills an event. They crushed this one and had raised the bar for themselves in the future. They had a fight cage set up, a dunk tank, a big-ass waterslide, and the food was off the chain. Brother Roundy and the Savannah good-time crew, hats off, brothers.

Friday evening was going to be special for me. Prospect Ox and a prospect he had gotten close with, Floki, from Jacksonville chapter had come to the end of their prospecting journey. It was a long hard road and today was their payday.

I performed their patching ceremony in front of all the brothers that attended the national. We closed off the backyard and kicked out any civilians, prospects, and ole ladies. I was just as excited for Ox as he was to being a patched member in this club. Like I said, Ox and I go back over a decade, and now we can participate in everything together. Very proud of you, brother. Love ya.

June 10, 2021. Myself and now patch-holder Ox headed to Southern Ohio again. We caged it due to severe storms and the cicada bug bullshit. I have to say, when we got to Ohio, we went through a couple areas on the highway where these things were blocking out the sun. When we got close to the clubhouse, we stopped for fuel, and those things were deafening. I wasn't too upset we didn't ride.

Southern Ohio received their MCs that night, and we all went to this blue bull or thirsty ball bull joint to eat. Ox and I turned and burned back home.

July 22, 2021. Ox and I rode out to Southern Ohio and spent the night there. In the morning, we all met up at the clubhouse with a few more out-of-state brothers, and we hit the highway to Southeast Kentucky for another scheduled presidents meeting. On the way, I wanted to see what these guys had for riding balls and gave them a

"Butta run." We were kicking it a hundred plus in a pack, terrorizing the civilians and making friends on the road! They all rode solid and kept up and in line.

Saturday we handled the business that needed to be handled. Then late Saturday afternoon we patched out the Southern Ohio probate chapter into the Wingmen nation! A lot of out-of-state brothers other than just presidents showed up for the occasion and again a very proud moment.

I watched these guys for the last almost four years give what they had to support this nation and to become Wingmen themselves. Hats off to all of you, brothers, and especially to Zach and Danny who were there from day one! Love all you guys and am very proud and honored to call you brothers.

August 1, 2021. I rode down to RB's house to hook up with him and head on down to see our brother Mike Roy in North Carolina. Mike had been diagnosed recently with terminal pancreatic cancer. There were a lot of brothers there. JD, Ninja Nic, Bobby Geico, Ditch, Johhny (if I missed any, I apologize), and of course, Mandy, his daughter, who hasn't left his side. We sat around and bullshitted and watched old movies and had pizza.

Mike Roy is a cornerstone in this club. He was there in the beginning in Italy and then in Fayetteville when he returned from Italy. He was a big part of writing our national bylaws. He served in every position at the chapter level. He served as our national president and national Chaplin as well. His mantra was "ride your bike and be a good brother." That is it in a nutshell, guys. It really is that simple.

What I love most about Mike Roy is, he will *always* tell it like he sees it. He has absolutely *zero* sugarcoating skills. If you don't want the truth, *don't* ask Mike! Mike talked to all. Didn't matter if you were a supporter, hang-around, prospect, three-day patch holder, or a lifer. Mike gave us his all, all the time.

Mike practically lived on his motorcycle. He loved to ride and did so every day. One of my fondest memories is he and I in Western North Carolina together. We went out early on a Saturday morning. We got breakfast at a local diner in Maggie Valley, then we spent the day at the motorcycle museum there and just riding the mountain roads. I love you, brother.

September 2, 2021. Ox and I headed down to Southeast Georgia for my last national as national president. I had gotten COVID a week or so prior and was on antibiotics and was nowhere near 100 percent, but there was no way I would miss this one or not ride to it. This would be my forty-fifth consecutive national I attended.

We got to the clubhouse, and I distanced myself from everyone just in case. It sucked, but I didn't know if I was still contagious, and I wasn't getting a COVID test. I only knew I had it 'cause I had the same symptoms as my wife, and she got tested.

So the next morning, Ox and I rolled down to Northwest Florida for the national. I addressed the nation one last time and passed the torch to Stew, who was voted in as our new national president, and Red Hooker Finch, who was voted in as our new national vice president.

Mike Roy was flown in by a charity organization that helps veterans. It was awesome to have him in attendance and have him open the meeting with his prayer. Sucked I couldn't give him a hug.

The nation had an awesome, big, flying W plaque made for me with all my years of service in the three different positions I held at the national level. It was bound in red-and-black leather with a sidearm and a handmade knife made by our brother, John Humphreys. The Devil's Elbow chapter had gotten and customized for me a 1974 Sportster chopper. (They owed me a bike! Story can't be told here.) It is awesome. It has five red eagles painted on it, with five of my closest brothers that have passed. Thank you again, brothers. I am honored. Brother Jason gave me a Wingmen nation ring on behalf of the Cherokee County chapter as well. And let's not forget the potato chips from the Oak Grove chapter! Ox and I rode home side by side, and the weather was just perfect.

This ends my most memorable trips for the year 2021 and brings this story to a close. I rode 8,954 miles, and I have visited out-of-state chapters twelve times.

CHAPTER 23

Advice to New Patch Holders

This is for any new patch holder in any club. If you joined a club for the right reasons in your heart, it will be one of the best things you do in your life. If you do it right and don't subject yourself to "new patch syndrome," it will be all the better. First and foremost, *do not turn into a drunken asshole after you patch*! Don't *ever* lie to a brother, *ever*, no matter how bad you may have fucked up. Take it on the chin! Men don't hide behind lies and/or excuses. I could live with a murderer before accepting a liar.

If you are going through some shit, don't be that macho guy who doesn't reach out for help. Why did you join a big organization for "brotherhood" if you won't accept a brother's help? Don't be a burden as well. Don't "expect" the club to always bail you out of stupid shit. Fix yourself and don't be a repeat offender. In other words, don't take advantage of your brother or the club. Be a man 24-7.

Don't worry about what someone else outside your chapter is doing unless it directly reflects on yourself. It is his chapter's responsibility to fix him. Don't be a "scorekeeper." Do what you do, and don't worry about who is doing less. Don't shit on a brother behind his back. If you can't or haven't said it to a brother's face, don't say it to anyone else first. If you have an issue, go to the wood line and handle your business like men.

This one is a new fad I see going on throughout the MC world and just chaps my ass. You *earn* status, reputation, road names, etc.

You don't create it for yourself. If you are trying to "stand out," why did you join a club with other "like-minded men"? You joined to be a member of that club and not to be an individual. If you need to stand out as an individual by doing stupid, dumb, "look at me" shit to boost your reputation, status, or ego, you probably shouldn't have joined a club. Your status and reputation are earned through putting in work, period. Earn that shit, new guy.

Be the best patch holder and brother you can be. Give more than you take. Be your brother's keeper, not his judge and jury. Earn your patch every single day.

EPILOGUE

I wanted to be a Wingmen to be a part of something bigger than myself and have many brothers to *Ride, Fight, Fuck, Drink, and Die* (RFFDD) with. Once I became a Wingmen, I wanted to give everything I could to ensure that good times would always be afforded for all Wingmen and make it as good as it gets for the ones that will come after me when I am gone. I dedicated the past fifteen years to this nation, giving 100 percent of myself 100 percent of the time. I held the positions of treasurer, sergeant of arms, vice president, and president at the local level. I held the positions of regional sergeant of arms, national sergeant of arms, vice president, and president at the national level. I rode a total of 284,585 miles, visiting out-of-state chapters (not including Rockland or Orange counties) 249 times with my eagle on my back. I like to say I have more miles backing to a curb then most men have going forward. I averaged 18,972 miles a year for fifteen years. I lost a lot and gained a lot in the process. I have few if any relationships outside this nation. I missed out on and took time and celebratory moments from my children and grandchildren. I declined multiple chances to be promoted at my job knowing it would hinder my dedication for the nation.

I believe I did make a difference in some brothers' lives, and hopefully, I helped strengthen this nation. I have adjusted my own fire in my life with the wisdom and advice that I had been given from brothers that care enough about me to share it with me. I have made irreplaceable relationships that I would have never had the chance to be a part of if I wasn't a Wingmen. I have met a lot of good people who have done me bad and a lot of bad people who treated me good. I have been shown unconditional brotherhood and have also seen it at its worst facade. It has been an awesome life experience being in these positions in the nation and has for sure been a roller coaster of a ride.

Again, thank you, brother Patrick Murphy. If not for you giving me the advice of keeping a "diary" of my trips, I am certain I wouldn't remember half of what I was able to write down and share with our brothers and future Wingmen. I thank God I made the decision to be a Wingmen every day.

Thank you, brother Mike Roy. If not for your vision and dedication, this thing may have never been. Thank you, brother, for fortifying my faith in times when I may have doubted it. You are a man's man and a true brother and friend. I know you are front right, leading the Ghost chapter.

My life now will be dedicated to being the best husband I can be to Jill and father/grandfather I can be. Though my kids are all adults now, these past couple years I have spent more and more time with my two youngest children and enjoy the time we have been spending together. I want to be with my wife and my dogs in our new RV (we just traded in the old one for a new 2022 toy hauler!) and travel this beautiful country that I love so much and see things I've only read about in books. I will remain a Wingmen the rest of my life and always make the club priority. I'll just do it at a different pace than I have been for the past fifteen years. I love my brothers. I love the Wingmen nation.

WFFW 9339 RFFDD Joey "Butta" WMC

ABOUT THE AUTHOR

Joey "Butta" Mazza is a fifty-seven-year-old blue-collar veteran workingman who belongs to the Wingmen Motorcycle Club. He is a hardworking, hard-playing, loyal friend and brother. He grew up in northeastern New Jersey where you have to have thick skin to survive. His loyalty and honesty are on another level. If you don't want the truth, do not ask him the question! This book is about his first fifteen years in the Wingmen Motorcycle Club, his rise in the ranks of leadership, and his crazy road trips with his brothers and civilian friends. He rode a little under three hundred thousand miles with his patch on his back over the last fifteen years. These are a few of the crazy road tales he has experienced. I hope you enjoy them as much as he enjoyed living them.

James Fonshill